DAVID TORRANC[...] a f[...] r[...], journalist and broadca[...] who specialises in th[...] [...]ory of the long-running deba[...] [...]out Scottish independence. After being educated in Edinburgh, Aberdeen and Cardiff he worked as a newspaper and television reporter before taking a brief career break to dabble in politics at Westminster. For the past seven years he has been a freelance commentator as well as the author or editor of more than ten books about Scottish and UK politics, biography and history. Like all good Scotsmen he has lived in London for long stretches, and is currently based there.

Luath Press in an independently owned and managed book publishing company based in Scotland and is not aligned to any political party or grouping. *Viewpoints* is an occasional series exploring issues of current and future relevance.

By the same author:

The Scottish Secretaries (Birlinn, 2006)
George Younger: A Life Well Lived (Birlinn, 2008)
'We in Scotland': Thatcherism in a Cold Climate (Birlinn, 2009)
Noel Skelton and the Property-Owning Democracy (Biteback, 2010)
Inside Edinburgh: Discovering the Classic Interiors of Edinburgh (Birlinn, 2010)
Salmond: Against the Odds (Birlinn, 2010)
Great Scottish Speeches I (ed.) (Luath Press, 2011)
David Steel: Rising Hope to Elder Statesman (Biteback, 2012)
Whatever Happened to Tory Scotland? (ed.) (Edinburgh University Press, 2012)
The Battle for Britain: Scotland and the Independence Referendum (Biteback, 2013)
Great Scottish Speeches II (ed.) (Luath Press, 2013)
100 Days of Hope and Fear: How Scotland's Referendum was Lost and Won (Luath Press, 2014)

Britain Rebooted

Why federalism would be good for the nations
and regions of the UK

DAVID TORRANCE

Luath Press Limited

EDINBURGH

www.luath.co.uk

First published 2014
Reprinted 2014
New edition 2015

ISBN: 978-1-910021-71-2

The author's right to be identified as author of this book
under the Copyright, Designs and Patents Act 1988 has been asserted.

The paper used in this book is recyclable. It is made from low chlorine pulps produced
in a low energy, low emission manner from renewable forests.

Printed and bound by Bell & Bain Ltd., Glasgow

Typeset in 11 point Sabon

© David Torrance 2014, 2015

For Sean Bye, whose knowledge of the dynamics of US federalism
was invaluable in preparing this book

Contents

Great Britain
(abbreviation: GB)
England, Wales, and Scotland considered as a unit. The name is also often used loosely to refer to the United Kingdom.

reboot
VERB
Restart or revive... give fresh impetus to...

federal
ADJECTIVE
Having or relating to a system of government in which several states form a unity but remain independent in internal affairs...

Federalism

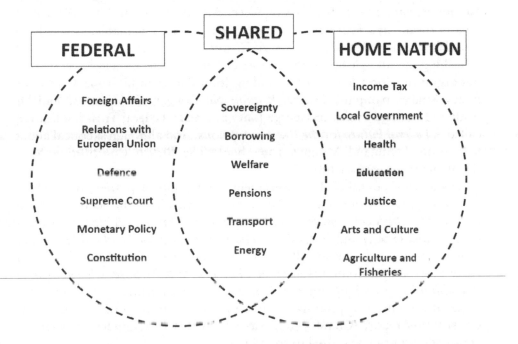

FEDERAL	SHARED	HOME NATION
Foreign Affairs	Sovereignty	Income Tax
Relations with European Union	Borrowing	Local Government
Defence	Welfare	Health
Supreme Court	Pensions	Education
Monetary Policy	Transport	Justice
Constitution	Energy	Arts and Culture
		Agriculture and Fisheries

Note on Sources

IN MY OTHER publications I have developed a habit of footnoting everything to within an inch of its life, but since this is a very different kind of book I have broken with that habit and eschewed references entirely. Nevertheless I must mention some of the texts on which I have drawn in the course of assembling my argument.

Two books by the Welsh Assembly Member David Melding, *Will Britain Survive Beyond 2020?* (Institute of Welsh Affairs, 2009) and *The Reformed Union: Britain as a Federation* (also IWA, 2013), were invaluable, as was John Kendle's excellent *Federal Britain: A History* (Routledge, 1997) in terms of refreshing my knowledge of the historical background. Others have also set out arguments for a federal UK including John Barnes in his 1998 Centre for Policy Studies pamphlet *Federal Britain: No Longer Unthinkable?* and Dr Andrew Blick and Professor George Jones in a 2010 Federal Trust publication called *A Federal Future for the UK: The Options*. And although skeptical about federalism, Ferdinand Mount's 1992 book *The British Constitution Now* (Heinemann) as very useful.

Documents published by governments and political parties, meanwhile, have also provided valuable material, especially two from the Scottish Liberal Democrats, *The Steel Commission: Moving to Federalism – A New Settlement for Scotland* (2005) and *Federalism: The Best Future for Scotland* (2012), as well as its successor, the so-called 'Campbell II' (2014). The Scottish Labour Party's Devolution Commission report, *Powers for a Purpose – Strengthening Accountability and Empowering People* (also 2014) echoed – to a degree – some of the Lib Dem proposals, while the 1973 Royal Commission on the Constitution report (Cmnd 5460) was an instructive reminder of what the anti-federalist argument used to sound like.

For the chapter on 'Educational Federalism' (which I accept might sit uneasily with the rest of the book), I drew upon the fourth 'Referendum' edition of the doorstopper *Scottish Education* (Edinburgh University Press, 2013), as well as Gerry Hassan's engagingly honest book *Caledonian Dreaming* (Luath, 2014), Jim Sillars' short book *In Place of Fear II* (Vagabond Voices, also 2014), George Walden's 1999 autobiography *Lucky George: Memoirs of an Anti-Politician* (Allen Lane), and extensively from two editions of the *New Statesman* dated 30 January and 6 February 2014.

Finally, the quotes in the opening chapter from Dean Acheson's curiously neglected (beyond one famous quote) speech come from *Vital Speeches of the Day*, Vol. XXIX, No. 6, dated 1 January 1963. Many other books, articles and websites are of course cited throughout the text and I have done my best to flag up the source in each instance.

Federalism Around the World

MORE THAN 25 countries around the world have a formally federal system of government. This is not a comprehensive list but illustrates that far from being uniform federations vary widely in shape, size and balance of powers. Not included are unitary states with regional government – however widespread – for example Spain, Indonesia, France and the Netherlands. These are not federal countries although, like the UK, they have federal characteristics.

ARGENTINA is a federation of 23 provinces and one autonomous city, Buenos Aires. Provinces hold all the power that they choose not to delegate to the federal government and under the Argentinian constitution they have to be representative but beyond this are fully autonomous, enacting their own constitutions and responsible for their own systems of local government and finances. Some provinces have bicameral legislatures, others unicameral. Each province has three seats in the federal Chamber of Senators.

AUSTRALIA is, like the United Kingdom, a parliamentary constitutional monarchy but with a federal division of powers. It has six states and three territories, including the Australian Capital Territory (ACT, which includes the capital of Canberra). Federal legislation can only over-ride state law in areas set out in Section 51 of the Australian constitution, otherwise state parliaments are responsible for all residual legislative powers, including those over schools, state police, the state judiciary, roads, public transport and local government. The federal Senate includes 12 senators from each state and two each from the territories.

AUSTRIA became a federal, parliamentary, democratic republic through its 1920 federal constitution, while the Second Republic – with its nine states – was re-enacted on 1 May 1945. Although Austria is a relatively small country (8.5 million people) it has nine states with legislative authority distinct from the federal government, for example in matters of culture, social care, youth and nature protection, hunting, building, and zoning ordinances. A president and chancellor govern at the federal level, while each state is represented in the Bundesrat.

BELGIUM is a constitutional monarchy and a federal parliamentary democracy. Constitutional revisions between 1970 and 1993 established a unique form of federalism with segregated political power at three levels: federal; 'language communities' (Flemish, French and German); and regions (Flemish, Walloon and Brussels-Capital). The federal government's authority includes justice, defence, federal police, social security, nuclear energy, monetary policy and public debt, and other aspects of public finances, while communities exercise their authority only within linguistically determined geographical boundaries. The federal Senate includes 21 representatives appointed by the three community parliaments.

BRAZIL is a federation composed of 26 states and one federal district, which includes the capital Brasilia. The states have autonomous administrations, collect their own taxes and receive a share of taxes collected by the federal government. They have a governor and a unicameral legislative body elected directly by their voters. They also have independent courts of law for common justice, although criminal and civil laws are a federal responsibility. The states and federal district each send three members to the federal Senate.

CANADA is a constitutional monarchy but also a federation composed of ten provinces and three territories. Provinces have more autonomy than territories, having responsibility for social programmes such as health care, education and welfare. while, taken together, the provinces collect more revenue than the federal government, an almost unique structure among world federations. Using its spending powers, the federal government can initiate policies at the provincial level, although the provinces can (but rarely do) opt out of these. Like the UK House of Lords, the federal Senate is appointed, albeit on a regional basis. The senate holds considerably less power than the House of Commons.

GERMANY comprises 16 states that are collectively referred to as Länder; each has its own constitution and is largely autonomous in relation to the federal government. The size and population of the states also varies considerably. Germany was constituted as a federal republic in 1949 and federal legislative power is vested in a parliament (the Reichstag) consisting of the Bundestag (federal diet) and Bundesrat (federal council), the latter consisting of representatives from the 16 federated states.

INDIA is a federation with a parliamentary system governed under the Indian constitution. It is composed of 28 states and seven 'union territories', most of which have elected legislatures and governments based on the Westminster model, although five of the territories are ruled directly via appointed administrators. In 1956 the states were reorganised on a linguistic basis and have remained largely unchanged since. Traditionally described as 'quasi-federal' given its initially strong centre and weak states, since the late 1990s India has grown increasingly federal as a result of political, economic, and social changes.

MALAYSIA is a federal constitutional monarchy closely modelled on the Westminster parliamentary system (though not, obviously, the federal bit). The head of state – or 'king' – is elected for a five-year term by and from the nine hereditary rulers of the Malay states (another four states with titular governors do not take part). Legislative power is divided between federal and state legislatures, the latter possessing unicameral assemblies led by chief ministers. The state assemblies elect 26 of 70 federal senators.

THE UNITED MEXICAN STATES are a federation under a presidential system of government. The constitution establishes three levels of government: the federal union, 31 'free and sovereign' state governments and municipal authorities. Each state has its own constitution, congress and judiciary and elects a governor for a six-year term. The federal district of Mexico City is a special political division belonging to the federation as a whole, while the federal Senate comprises 128 senators, half of which are elected by each State (two each, as in the USA).

RUSSIA is a very large, and therefore very complicated, federation comprising 85 federal 'subjects', to which the republic of Crimea and the federal city of Sevastopol were recently added. These subjects each have two delegates in the Federation Council although the degree of autonomy they enjoy varies depending on their status: oblasts (or provinces, of which there are 46), republics (22), krais (or territories, nine), autonomous okrugs (or districts, four), together with a Jewish Autonomous Oblast and three federal cities (Moscow, St Petersburg and Sevastopol).

SWITZERLAND's federal constitution adopted by Switzerland in 1848 makes it among the world's oldest. Although a new constitution was adopted in 1999 it did not alter a federal structure dividing powers between the confederation and 26 cantons. These possess a permanent constitutional status and a high degree of independence with their own constitutions, parliaments, governments and courts. Each is represented in the federal Council of States.

THE UNITED STATES is the world's oldest surviving federation with the US Constitution regulating its government via a system of checks and balances. There are three levels of government: federal, state and local, with 50 states (the most recent being Hawaii, which joined in 1959) and the District of Columbia (which contains the capital of Washington, DC), together with five overseas territories. The states, which vary considerably in terms of size and population, each send two members to the federal US Senate. States do not have the right to unilaterally secede from the Union, which also observes the tribal sovereignty of the 'native nations'.

Introduction to the 2015 Edition

IT WAS PERHAPS the most dramatic moment of the long independence referendum campaign. Late on Saturday 6 September details emerged of a YouGov opinion poll that put the Yes campaign in the lead for the first time. At around the same time the *Observer*'s splash went online and, strikingly, it included the 'f' word.

'The people of Scotland', it read, 'are to be offered a historic opportunity to devise a federal future for their country before next year's general election.' A devolution announcement was to be made within days, and in the event of a No vote Scots were to be consulted on further transfers of power from London to Holyrood.

Former Liberal Democrat leader Sir Menzies Campbell told the *Observer* it was 'a remarkable opportunity... to create a relationship with the rest of the UK which to all intents and purposes would be federal', while the paper's regular columnist Will Hutton said Westminster's party leaders 'must offer to create a federal Britain', what he called 'a wholesale recasting of the British state', including 'a second chamber that represents all parts of the federation'.

Hutton at least understood that the key to delivering British federalism lay in England and the Upper House rather than solely with Scotland, unlike the un-named individual who had briefed the 'f' word to a Sunday newspaper. Devolving more powers to Scotland in the event of a No vote would not, of course, necessarily constitute federalism, although the fact it had entered the Whitehall lexicon was significant in itself.

When the first edition of this book was published in the spring of 2014 it was regarded, predictably, as a bit eccentric, as most talk of federalism in a UK context usually is. Reviewing it (and Linda Colley's *Acts of Union and Disunion*) in the *Irish Times*, Gerry Hassan argued that in the absence of any interest south of the border in an English parliament or regionalism then 'all such plans, whether from Colley and Torrance or various think tanks, are merely liberal-elite wish fulfilment'.

But as referendum day approached – and the opinion polls narrowed – federalism moved from the fringes of the independence debate to the mainstream, with newspaper editorials, columnists and, increasingly, opposition politicians all deploying the term, the most prominent of which was former Prime Minister Gordon Brown, whose book *My Scotland, Our Britain* was a federalist manifesto in all but name. As he concluded in the *Guardian*, if his programme (regional English assemblies, a UK Senate and a written constitution) was implemented then within two years of a No vote there would exist 'a system of government as close to federalism as you can have in a nation where one part forms 85 per cent of the population'.

Later Alex Salmond, Nicola Sturgeon *et al* deliberately took this quote out of context to imply that Brown believed the so-called 'Vow', as set out in the *Daily Record*, if implemented, would amount to a federal settlement for Scotland in the UK. But 'more powers' or 'devo-max' for Scotland was not, as some commentators appeared to believe, the same as a federal UK. Others, for example the Tory-aligned constitutional lawyer Adam Tomkins and the civil servant-turned-Labour adviser Jim Gallagher, argued for wide-ranging constitutional reform but flinched from using the 'f' word.

Chairing an Edinburgh International Book Festival event with the historian Linda Colley during August 2014, the veteran journalist Magnus Linklater expressed the orthodox view that federalism was 'alien' to the 'British tradition'. Rightly, Colley did not accept this point, later adding: 'When people say: "we couldn't do it", are people in these islands really that stupid?' This got a reasonable round of applause, which was heartening, but then as the blogger Rory Scothorne concluded in his online review of *Britain Rebooted*, federalist arguments generally deserved better than the usual 'lazy impossibilist critiques'. Strikingly, even self-styled constitutional 'radicals' suddenly became conservatives when federalism was flagged up as a serious alternative to their preferred option of independence.

Of course, creating a truly federal UK, even in light of the No vote, remained easier said than done. A UK-wide constitutional convention was regularly mooted, not least by the Labour Party, while I put my name to a couple of letters to *The Times* (signed by a wide range of civic figures as well as lowly journalists) calling for precisely that. In response William Hague, the Leader of the House, was not wholly dismissive, while a subsequent Command Paper on *The Implications of Devolution for England* sounded almost positive, although it made the point that encompassing already extant constitutional reform might not be practical. The Liberal Democrats, who gathered for their annual conference shortly after the referendum, also debated and passed a motion to 'empower' a convention to 'produce a new written constitution for a Federal United Kingdom, and to further shape new institutions for England'.

The Lib Dem motion ('Towards a Federal UK') argued that the No vote allowed the 'creation of the fully Federal UK long advocated by Liberals and Liberal Democrats'. Furthermore, it called for the delivery of the 'Vow' promised before the referendum, implementation of the Silk Commission recommendations in Wales, and the introduction of a 'Devolution Enabling Bill' at Westminster, facilitating 'devolution on demand' in England via the transfer of legislative powers from the UK Parliament to councils or groups of councils.

Interestingly, an organisation called the Society of Conservative Lawyers also published a paper called 'Our Quasi Federal Kingdom', an attempt to cast federalism within a long-standing 'Tory tradition' of incremental constitutional reform. It concluded that the UK Parliament ought to pass a 'Statute of Union' declaring the United Kingdom to be 'a quasi-federal, voluntary union of England, Scotland, Wales and Northern Ireland'. This the Society saw going hand in hand with the devolution of 'full territorial competence' to the Welsh Assembly, more devolution for Scotland along the lines of the Strathclyde Commission and 'English Votes for English Laws' as per the McKay Commission. Finally, it also advocated an annual 'UK summit' chaired by the Prime Minister and opened by the Queen. Andrew Rosindell, a Conservative MP, also introduced his 'Parliamentary and Constitutional Reform Bill' under the 10-minute-rule procedure in November 2014 (supported by Labour, Plaid Cymru and SNP MPs), calling for a federal system similar to that of Australia or Canada.

Professor Stephen Tierney from the University of Edinburgh even went so far as to suggest it was 'not too dramatic to say that federalism may well be the last throw of the dice for the Anglo-Scottish union', his argument being that 'only a federal system' could manage changes such as those outlined in the Smith Commission (see below) 'while also giving Scotland a continuing stake in the Union'. 'Otherwise,' he judged, 'as the Scottish Parliament gets stronger and stronger, the UK will appear more and more irrelevant to many Scots.' Meanwhile Tory grandee Lord Salisbury, a former Leader of the House of Lords, floated the idea of a federal state in which the House of Commons became the English Parliament, while the House of Lords would be abolished to make way for, as the journalist Charles Moore put it, an 'elected Parliament of the entire United Kingdom, dealing only with those matters – defence, foreign policy, national budget etc – which are not devolved'. The Prime Minister, necessarily, would be a member of the latter body.

But holistic 'federal' or 'quasi-federal' schemes remained the exception: UK constitutional reform had always tended to be piecemeal, and so it remained. Labour leader Ed Miliband, for example, picked up Gordon Brown's proposal for making the 'second chamber of [the UK] Parliament truly a Senate of the Regions and Nations of our whole country', as part of a new constitutional settlement produced by a constitutional convention shortly after the next general election.

This was pretty radical stuff, although another strand of Miliband's constitutional agenda – devolution to the English regions – was less successful. Even Jon Cruddas, the head of Labour's policy review, admitted that his party had not been as 'agile' as the Conservatives when it came to dealing with the elephant in the room (i.e. England). Cruddas was referring to Chancellor George Osborne's plans to create a new mayor for Greater Manchester and grant further powers to the region as part of his drive to create a 'northern powerhouse'.

This was later followed up with a deal for Sheffield and Leeds, which was to be given similar autonomy but without (unlike Greater Manchester) an elected mayor. The crucial element was that both proposals involved 'combined' local authorities, which the UK Government, and indeed Labour, seemed to regard as their preferred model for regional English devolution, nascent city-regions which removed the need for new (and undoubtedly expensive) devolved assemblies. Joe Anderson, the Mayor of Liverpool, also said the case for devolution to other 'combined' authorities like those in Merseyside was 'a powerful one and should be recognised', even though not all the councils concerned agreed.

Such schemes recognised a growing demand from among English civic leaders, not just local authority chiefs in Manchester and Yorkshire but also the veteran Sir Albert Bore in Birmingham, for greater devolution both before and after the Scottish independence referendum. 'As more powers and new ways of working are devolved to other parts of the union,' wrote the leaders of the 'combined' Greater Manchester authorities to the *Guardian* in early October 2014, 'this position [the region lacking any formal devolution] becomes untenable.' They argued that Greater Manchester was ideally placed to be a 'trailblazer for city devolution' with decision-making around skills and training, welfare and employment, transport, health and social care all being transferred to the combined authorities.

Jim O'Neil, a former chief economist at Goldman Sachs, who headed up the Royal Society of Arts' City Growth Commission, largely agreed with Civic England. His report, 'Unleashing Metro Growth', concluded that more power should be devolved to city regions in tandem with greater devolution for Scotland. On one level this degree of activity (and consensus) was surprising, for as the first edition of this book noted several English cities had rejected directly-elected mayors in 2012, as had the North East a regional assembly in 2004.

So what had changed? Some argued that the lively (and lengthy) debate over Scottish independence had increased public interest in devolution, although 'Future of England' report 'Taking England Seriously: The New English Politics' concluded (yet again) that there was little appetite in England (among voters if not their civic leaders) for more devolution either to regions or local councils. It depended, of course, how the question was framed, for a separate BBC ComRes poll found that 80 per cent of the English supported having more powers devolved to local areas. Dr Mark Stuart of the University of Nottingham said appetite for devolution had been a 'growing trend' and although people were still split on the idea of an English parliament support had grown over the past decade. 'I think people in northern England, for example,' he said, 'are seeing how the referendum has benefited Scotland and they want a share of the pie.'

The only proposals that attracted a degree of unanimity and, importantly, salience, were those loosely categorised as 'English Votes for English Laws'. As Prime Minister David Cameron put it on the steps of Downing Street early on 19 September 2014: 'We have heard the voice of Scotland — and now the millions of voices of England must also be heard. The question of English votes for English laws, the so-called West Lothian question requires a decisive answer.' Only English Votes for English Laws, inevitably boiled down to the unfortunate acronym 'EVEL', struck many (including this author) as the wrong answer to the right question: how was England to be governed within the UK?

Although the Prime Minister deserved (but did not get) credit for at least trying to make a hitherto exclusively Scottish debate more holistic in nature, there were obvious problems with creating, in essence, two classes of MPs, particularly from a Unionist perspective, even the EVEL-lite option set out by William Hague in February 2015. Cameron did so, however, largely to close down a growing backbench rebellion led by John Redwood, who had erected the straw man of an English parliament. Speaking to *Newsnight*, however, Cameron said he did not believe the political dynamic was 'remotely' close to that sort of development.

The Smith Commission, which reported three days early on 27 November 2014, provoked the usual careless talk about federalism (*The Times*' splash screamed, inexplicably, 'Fears of a federal UK as Scots get new powers'), and although many of its recommendations hinted at an increasingly federal relationship between the UK's central government at Westminster and its four devolved assemblies or parliaments (together with moves to make Holyrood 'permanent'), it amounted to greater devolution for Scotland rather than a wholesale recasting of the famously unwritten British constitution.

So Smith was not some sort of unilateral federalism, and although it arguably delivered upon the 'Vow' (at least as set out in the *Daily Record*), at the same time it exacerbated all the tensions, chiefly Barnett and the West Lothian Question (the 'two mad men in the attic' as Professor Iain McLean called them), of the existing devolution settlement. Simply devolving 'more powers' in an *ad hoc* fashion was also subject to the law of diminishing political returns. Selling largely technical (and, it has to be said, academic) changes had proved difficult in the past (Calman) and would no doubt do so again. In that context, the 'Vow Plus' promised by Gordon Brown and Scottish Labour leader Jim Murphy in the run-up to the 2015 general election looked desperate as well as incoherent.

Only a properly federal settlement for the whole of the UK, as I argued in the original edition of *Britain Rebooted*, could possibly hope to succeed, and if Unionists are serious about preserving the UK then the future can only be bright if it's federal. As Stephen Tierney, Professor of Constitutional Theory at the University of Edinburgh, put it: 'only a federal system can manage these changes while also giving Scotland a continuing stake in the Union.'

But whatever happens post-Smith, and its recommendations could of course be subject to the law of unintended consequences, significantly, post-referendum the 'f' word is now mainstream, so much so that even Nationalists deploy it in debate, and not always in a pejorative sense. Indeed, the logic of Nicola Sturgeon *et al* criticising Smith for not delivering 'near federalism' (as implied by Gordon Brown) was that if it had been then they would have been content.

But as Alasdair McKillop argued in his LSE review of *Britain Rebooted*, however neat federalist arguments are, 'serious questions remain over how the political and, crucially, popular momentum will be generated to carry the UK to [a] federal future'. Is that future now more likely post-referendum? I would say yes. But how likely is that? Alas, still not very. Even the pro-independence Jamie Maxwell, writing in the *Scottish Review of Books*, acknowledged that federalism 'probably would be the *neatest* of the available constitutional options', in certain respects 'the most practical – and in some ways distinctively *British* – choice', although he remained understandably cynical that such a choice would come to pass.

In an important column for the *Guardian* in early 2015 the historian Timothy Garton Ash pondered how the UK would respond to a typically messy constitutional picture if it were in fact German. They would, he wrote, 'address both sides of the question by an explicit, logical set of constitutional arrangements, specifying what is to be done at each level: European, federal (British), constituent nation (England, Scotland, Wales, Northern Ireland), regional, city, local'. Personally, added Garton Ash, 'I think this is where we should be aiming to end up, with a Federal Kingdom of Britain inside a confederal EU'.

To repeat, no system of governance is perfect, how could it be in such a complex and ever-changing world? As Dr Matt Qvortrup observed in his politely critical *Scotsman* review, federalism has rarely 'resolved matters pertaining to nationalist sentiment', for example in Belgium and Canada, and that is certainly true, although my arguments *for* a federal settlement (hopefully) go beyond simple containment of Scottish Nationalism.

Fittingly, I began writing this introduction to the new edition of *Britain Rebooted* in New York City, where debate about an increasingly dysfunctional federal settlement was in full swing. As Dr Qvortrup also observed, in the United States the motto *E pluribus unam* ('out of many one') has become almost an article of faith and not, often, a very helpful one. To quote John Quincy Adams II following the American Civil War: 'You are come so that once more we may pledge ourselves to a new union, not a union merely of law, or simply of the lips: ... of the sword, but gentlemen, the only true union, the union of hearts.'

Adams, of course, was addressing the Southern – rather than the Scottish – Question. Nevertheless in the wake of an altogether more peaceful (and democratic) revolution, the UK still has an opportunity to craft a more perfect union. As the BBC journalist Allan Little put it in a *Panorama* documentary just before polling day, future generations of Scots will 'need reasons to love and trust the Union as our parents and grandparents did, rather than simply to fear the alternative'. I am more convinced than ever before that the most likely route to that perhaps quixotic destination remains a federal one.

David Torrance
www.davidtorrance.com
@davidtorrance
London, March 2015

Foreword

Seeking a Role

ON 5 DECEMBER 1962, out of office for a decade but still a major figure in international affairs, the former Secretary of State Dean Acheson addressed an audience at the United States Military Academy at West Point, New York. Great Britain, he famously remarked in the course of his speech, had 'lost an empire' but 'not yet found a role'. Its 'attempt to play a separate power role' apart from Europe, a role based on a 'special relationship' with the US, a role based on being head of a Commonwealth with 'no political structure, or unity, or strength' was, he added, 'about played out'.

And in its attempt to 'work alone and to be a broker between the United States and Russia', Acheson reckoned the UK had 'seemed to conduct policy as weak as its military power'. For Harold Macmillan, the Anglo-Scottish Prime Minister of that empire-less and role-less nation, it hurt to hear this from the Anglophile Acheson (whose father, an Anglican priest, had been born in England) largely because it was true. Writing in his diary, Macmillan thought Acheson had always been 'a conceited ass', but conceded that the generally prickly response to his speech had not been 'a good sign, for we ought to be strong enough to laugh off this kind of thing'. In his formal response, meanwhile, Macmillan stressed the doctrine of 'interdependence' in post-war affairs.

But with the benefit of more than three decades observing US and international affairs, Acheson had identified an uncomfortable truth about the post-war UK. In the early 1960s it was in the process of shedding, rather than losing, its empire and was still, as Acheson's infamous epigram more accurately identified, searching for a role. Even more humiliatingly, within months of the speech Charles de Gaulle would veto the UK's application (one he thought wise) to join the fledgling Common Market, depriving it of an alternative European role. As Acheson had anticipated, that 'battle' seemed 'about as hard-fought as were those of an earlier day'.

And while Acheson's remarks were intended for the UK as a whole (his use of 'Great Britain' was in itself revealing) they also unconsciously applied to Scotland, for in 1962, a few months before the speech, the SNP had first emerged as a modern electoral force, polling nearly 10,000 votes in the West Lothian by-election. Appropriately enough, the Labour victor in that fight, Tam Dalyell, would later best articulate the tensions implicit in the UK's attempt to find an internal role as well as an external one, the so-called 'West Lothian Question' and all that flowed from it.

The decline of Great Britain and the rise of the SNP, as various political scientists have charted, was not unrelated. By the 1960s there was a sense, politically, economically and culturally, that the Union – that of 1707 rather than 1801 – was no longer delivering for Scotland. Not only did Westminster and its leaders look tweedy and out-of-date (as Acheson had also observed of post-war French and German leaders), but the Scottish economy had been diverging markedly from the rest of the UK in the decades since the First World War. The Union, largely unquestioned in the 18th and 19th centuries, no longer looked beyond reproach.

And while aspects of that decline were subsequently addressed, via legislative devolution and economic policies that brought the Scottish economy – certainly by the late 1980s – into phase with the UK as a whole, it never amounted to a holistic and sustainable solution to problems both perceived and real. Devolution, always ad hoc and often politically opportunistic, was a sticking plaster rather than a delicately executed operation.

Acheson's speech ('Our Atlantic Alliance') had focused on the 13-year-old North Atlantic Treaty Organisation (NATO), but he clearly saw Western Europe – in political and military terms – developing along federal lines, referring to 'progress toward integration... which has been going on for over a decade'. 'The forces which these far-seeing and imaginative policies have set in motion', he added, 'are surely the constructive forces of the future, upon which we must base both our hopes and our policy.' Acheson continued:

> Furthermore, we know from our own experience, an experience which is born out by that of other federal states, that federalism never stands still. It either moves towards increasing strength, increasingly managed by the central authority, or it tends to weaken and disintegrate. If the latter can be prevented, the former will surely occur.

But Acheson warned against seeking solutions in machinery alone, noting that institutions of government in themselves 'amount to little; importance lies in the extent and solidity of the agreements as to what they are to do'.

He also acknowledged that such solutions were difficult although not impossible, quoting the great French political thinker Alexis de Tocqueville, who saw that a democracy 'can only with great difficulty regulate the details of an important undertaking, persevere with a fixed design, and work out its execution in spite of serious obstacles'. With that, Acheson urged those in Western Europe to 'increase the tempo of action', concluding with a quote from President Lincoln in 1862: 'The occasion is piled high with difficulty, and we must rise with the occasion.'

Half a century on, and with Europe in similar (if less destructive) flux, much of Acheson's wisdom applies to a United Kingdom now shorn of all but the detritus of empire and accustomed to a clearer, if less than perfect, role in an increasingly interdependent world. It is a world that neither offers easy solutions to a myriad of challenges, nor a clear route map towards greater equality and happier, more co-operative states, not to forget component parts of states. In 2014, with an independence referendum due on 18 September, the occasion is, as Lincoln observed of post-Civil War America, piled high with difficulty, and thus it demands not only Scotland but the rest of the UK to rise to the occasion.

Which brings me to federalism, a view, although currently a minority one, that has the prospect of attracting wide support, from Nationalist to Unionist, Left to Right, and pretty much everything in between. As Alex Bell, a former policy chief to the SNP Scottish Government, observed, 'if Britain were to listen to its citizens again, it could become an astonishing model of how the world will organise itself perhaps for the next century or so'. Had the UK moved to give parity to each British nation or region, he added, then 'we would have become the first cluster of nations to rethink their shared purpose in the 21st century. We could be pioneers precisely in the way that the original union was a pioneer in 1707.'

Bell couched his remarks in the past tense, as he clearly believed no such re-imagining of the UK was in prospect any time soon. I do not share his (understandable) cynicism, for even if a federal solution does not enjoy ostentatious support, it could be argued that it exists implicitly, given succour by a general sentiment that constitutional ad hocery is unsustainable. Not only is there a lively ongoing debate in London, Wales, Northern Ireland and of course Scotland about 'more powers', even in hitherto constitutionally conservative England there is at last serious discussion of localism, city-based regionalism and breaking the dominance of Whitehall. Sure, a lot of this discourse is untidy and lacks coherence, but neither the status quo nor independence represents the logical end point of those discussions.

Therefore I unapologetically posit a rebooted, federal UK as a constitutional Middle Way I am sure Harold Macmillan would have approved of were he still active in politics today. It is a pragmatic recognition that neither Unionist nor

Nationalist enjoys a monopoly of wisdom, and indeed a federal UK offers the best chance of achieving an institutional rapprochement between those two often-hostile forces. In that context the referendum debate has been useful, for it has afforded a good – perhaps the only – opportunity to put the UK's constitutional house in order.

But as Dean Acheson recognised, it is not enough to propose purely mechanical changes in order to bring about better outcomes. A federal UK can only ever be a means to an end, not an end in itself. Since the 1960s Scottish political discourse has too often regarded constitutional change as a sort of panacea, and it has frequently become a means by which to avoid difficult policy decisions. Thus this short tract cautiously offers some suggested reforms in other areas, chiefly in the realms of local government, economics, welfare and education.

I do not mind admitting that doing so makes me a little uneasy. Should a journalist and mere commentator set out not only constitutional models but policy prescriptions? For a long time I would have answered 'no'; journalists ought to comment and analyse, not suggest remedies. But today the boundaries are so often blurred that I see no reason to be squeamish about such things. Too much of a commentator's life can involve the practice of (modest) power without responsibility, so why not get one's hands dirty for a change?

Pigeonholing this prospectus – a dogmatic habit to which Scottish politics is prone – will be intentionally difficult. Federalism is, generally speaking, a Liberal or Liberal Democrat goal, although one (as I will argue) with a slightly broader ideological provenance, while my thinking on certain policy areas is an undoubtedly muddled mix of Left, Right and everything in between. Although I was briefly involved with the Scottish Conservative Party as a student (no one could accuse me of being a careerist), I was on the Tory Reform Group wing of the party and never particularly comfortable as a party hack.

I have always been ecumenical in political terms, willing to see positives in most parties or movements, a tendency exacerbated by more than a decade as a professional observer of the political game. To me nothing sums this up better than Otto von Bismarck's aphorism that politics is 'the art of the possible'. So there is little point trying to categorise what follows as 'conservatism', 'socialism' (as Jim Sillars has done) and, worst of all, 'social democracy', for such labels lead nowhere particularly useful.

Rather this is the highly personal perspective of someone born in the summer of 1977, when – according to recent surveys – the UK was at its most equal and therefore also its happiest. It was an era of genuine social security, relatively cheap housing, relatively abundant jobs and relatively good social mobility. It is also the perspective of someone who could be said, although such things are inevitably subjective, to have moved from working to middle class in the course of his life. But while it is tempting to look to the past in pursuit of solutions, both constitutional and otherwise, it is something I hope I have resisted.

Nor do I make grandiose claims for either the achievability of federalism or what it might facilitate in policy terms. On such things I tend to be cautious and, as will come as no surprise to those who know me well, cynical. Like David Melding in his two excellent books on British federalism (with which the present volume cannot hope to compete), I am not seeking to present an unanswerable case for a UK federation but rather to show that, contrary to the opinion of many, a federal UK *is* possible.

I finished writing this while travelling through Central America which, alas, is not a good advert for federalism. Constituted in 1823, the Federal Republic of Central America lasted just 15 years, dissolving after a series of bloody conflicts. As the next chapter will set out, Great Britain or the UK has also toyed with federalism in its three century-long history. I can only agree with the sentiments of the political writer David Marquand who asked rhetorically: 'Does the UK become a federal state, or does it break up?' 'It would be nice to think', he replied to himself, 'we shall do better than our great grandparents did.' Amen to that.

David Torrance
Edinburgh and London, April 2014

CHAPTER I

A Short History of UK Federalism

THE IDEA OF a federal Britain is actually as old as Britain – or rather Great Britain – itself. During the debates in the early 18th century about the proposed Union between Scotland and England, numerous addresses were submitted to the old Scots parliament arguing not so much *against* unification but rather its 'incorporating' nature. The great patriot Andrew Fletcher of Saltoun was among those who argued that an 'incorporating union' would amount to a step too far.

Therefore Fletcher pressed for better terms and, in a series of influential speeches in 1703, argued that any future monarch's powers ought to be qualified by the Scottish Parliament's power to appoint ministers, raise a military force, approve taxation, and so on. Known as the 'twelve limitations', they drew upon the conditions imposed by the 1641 Scots parliament on Charles I, but Fletcher also intended to reinvent – or reboot in modern parlance the century old Union of the Crowns (not really a union at all, the two kingdoms remaining separate) along more federal lines in order to protect Scotland's nationhood.

Although undoubtedly eloquent, Fletcher lost that particular battle and when the terms of the Treaty of Union were published in 1706 he could not believe Scots would accept them, and indeed rioting the following year perhaps indicated they, unlike their political masters, did not. Thereafter Fletcher abandoned politics, dying (ironically) in London in 1716, his last coherent words, as reported by his nephew to his brother, being 'Lord have mercy upon my poor countrey that is so barbarously oppressed'.

Somewhat inevitably, Fletcher was eventually claimed by Scottish Nationalists as an early patriot firmly opposed to any sort of Union with England although John Morrison Davidson, in an 1880s pamphlet for the Scottish Home Rule Association, was careful to present him as an exemplary proto-federalist, 'equally opposed to separation and incorporation'.

And although incorporating union went ahead, Great Britain did have federal features, with distinct arrangements for its church, legal system and educational institutions. Following another Act of Union in 1801, meanwhile, Great Britain, now rebranded the 'United Kingdom of Great Britain and Ireland', acquired another territorially distinct component to the west.

Indeed Ireland's treatment as a distinctive unit within the UK, even after formal Union in the early 19th century, with a separate administration (echoed in Scotland with the creation of the Scottish Office in 1885) was unique within the British Empire. Although far from a formal federation, even then the UK was comfortably incorporating different institutions and territorial considerations in a quasi-federal manner. In fact, an early commentator on federalism, Edward Freeman, argued that to be 'of any value' a Federal Union had to 'arise by the establishment of a closer tie between elements which were before distinct, not by the division of members which have been hitherto more closely united'.

In other words, federalism might have worked in 1707 and 1801 but not thereafter. As Freeman wrote in 1863: 'No one could wish to cut up our United Kingdom into a federation, to invest English Counties with the rights of American States, or even to restore Scotland and Ireland to the quasi-Federal position which they held before their respective Unions.' Yet even as Freeman wrote those words (his skepticism set a benchmark for the next century or so), the UK had been willing – at least since the 1840s – to use federalism, as the historian John Kendle put it, as a means of 'ensuring economic, strategic and political stability in the white settlement colonies of British North America, New Zealand, Australia and South Africa'.

By the 1860s British colonial officials were encouraging British North Americans to unite along federal lines, and in 1867 the Dominion of Canada became the first federation within the British Empire, followed in 1901 by the Commonwealth of Australia. Even the federal constitution of the United States had been created several decades earlier by (formerly) British citizens influenced above all by British political ideas, not least a two-chamber parliamentary system. So the obvious question, posed by Kendle, was 'why did the British readily adopt the federal idea in the empire but not at home?' The answer, he posited, seemed 'to lie in a reluctance of the political elite to share power – to divide sovereignty – within the United Kingdom'. The British, therefore, 'proceeded with impunity to 'invent' federal structures abroad but to spurn the concept at home'.

This dogma, whose high priest was the constitutional theorist AV Dicey, held sway for the next few decades, enduring even after it was weakened from the mid-19th century onwards not just through federal developments in the Empire but more acutely between 1886 and 1922 because of the Irish Question. Famously in thrall to the idea of Parliamentary sovereignty, Dicey proclaimed (not inaccurately) that under the British constitution the 1707 Act of Union was of no greater authority than the Dentists Act of 1878. He was therefore appalled by federalism as he (correctly) believed it would require a written constitution, a superior court, a formal distribution of powers and an Irish parliament. It would, he concluded melodramatically in an 1882 article, 'dislocate every English [sic] constitutional arrangement'. As he elaborated:

> [Federalism] revolutionises the whole constitution of the United Kingdom; by undermining the parliamentary sovereignty, it deprives English institutions of their elasticity, their strength, and their life; it weakens the Executive at home, and lessens the power of the country to resist foreign attack. The revolution which works these changes holds out no hope of conciliation with Ireland. An attempt, in short, to impose on England and Scotland a constitution which they do not want, and which is quite unsuited to the historical traditions and to the genius of Great Britain, offers to Ireland a constitution which Ireland is certain to dislike, which has none of the real or imaginary charms of independence, and ensures none of the solid benefits to be hoped for from a genuine union with England.

But as John Kendle noted, what most concerned Dicey was 'English power and English sovereignty'. Not only did 'he pass quickly over the heterogeneity of the British state but he paid no heed to the complex regional mix within England'. But of course more than Diceyan dogma prevented a UK federation moving beyond the drawing board at this point in time, without a groundswell of public support for federalism, judged Kendle, 'no politicians and certainly no political party would waste time on its promotion. No political exigency equalled [sic] no political action.'

Within an Irish context, federalism enjoyed marginally more traction. The Nationalist politician Isaac Butt promoted it in the 1870s, advocating domestic parliaments for not only Ireland but also Scotland and England (he did not mention Wales). This inclination to square the circle of the Irish Question was later taken up by William Gladstone – after 1886 the main proponent of Irish Home Rule – as a penumbra intended to resolve some standard objections to Irish devolution. Although explicitly *anti*-federalist, what became known as 'Home Rule All Round' (which would have left the UK looking a little like post-Franco Spain in constitutional terms) did little to appease 'Unionists', those in the Conservative and Liberal parties who regarded any concession as a slippery slope to the disintegration of not only the UK but the wider British Empire.

But at the same time there was barely a cigarette paper between 'Home Rule All Round' and formal federalism and indeed the terms were often used interchangeably. Both visions also enjoyed support from prominent figures, not just the Grand Old Man but politicians like Joseph Chamberlain, who also backed the quixotic ideal of 'Imperial Federation', a possibility which, in the latter decades of the 19th century and well into the 1920s, was endlessly explored, examined and discussed. Between 1910 and 1914, meanwhile, the idea of federating the UK was taken much more seriously due to renewed consideration of the Irish Question, which – at the third time of asking – had become louder and therefore more urgent.

David Lloyd George, not yet Prime Minister, and Winston Churchill, at that point in the Liberal phase of his career, were enthusiastic, with the latter suggesting in a 1912 speech in Dundee that a workable federal system could only be established in the UK if England was divided into as many as ten or twelve self-governing areas. But such talk, as Harold Cox, editor of the *Edinburgh Review*, observed perceptively in July 1918, was largely reactive, with most British politicians promoting federalism 'primarily because they think it would settle the Irish problem, not because they have seriously considered the merits of federalism from the point of view of England, or even of Scotland or Wales'. Cox thought that in 'their mouths federalism is little more than a phrase employed for the purpose of avoiding the hard facts of the real Irish problem' which, to him, was 'essentially a question of nationality'.

This was a reasonable analysis, while in any case the outbreak of the Great War a few months later brought such talk to an abrupt end, along with the third Irish Home Rule Bill, which entered purgatory despite having cleared Parliament. But however traumatic, the war to end all wars did not, of course, answer the Irish Question, nor did it kill off the dreams of federalists. As ever, the latter developed in tandem with the former, and between 1919 and 1920 UK federalism reached its high watermark, with even a Cabinet sub-committee tasked with drafting a Bill for a federal UK that would square off Nationalist aspirations with (Ulster) Unionist fears. One Unionist candidate even fought the 1918 general election in the Scottish constituency of Bothwell advocating 'the general principle of all-round Devolution or Federation, so as to relieve the Imperial Parliament of the consideration of many matters which could be better dealt with by Federal Legislatures'.

Chairing that committee, meanwhile, was Walter Long, First Lord of the Admiralty, who had moved from staunch opponent of Irish Home Rule to persistent advocate of a federal settlement. At work, he displayed all the zeal of the convert, but as is so often the case in politics he was at the mercy of unfolding events, and although his work was not completely wasted, ultimately it applied only to Northern and Southern Ireland via the 1920 Government of Ireland Act, which essentially applied federal principles to one half of the United Kingdom. That solution was also was overtaken by events, chiefly the Irish Nationalists' refusal to recognise the Southern Irish parliament. By 1922 (the year in which A.V. Dicey died), the Irish Free State had been born and the Northern Irish parliament – Stormont, equipped with considerable autonomy – settled down to a quasi-federal relationship with mainland Great Britain.

In its Campaign Guide for the 1950 general election the Conservative Party likened the position of Stormont vis-à-vis the UK with 'the federal structures of Canada and Australia, where the separate states possess considerable powers of local autonomy, but are represented in the central dominion Parliament which retains the control of essential major matters'. It added:

> So it is with Northern Ireland. Her Parliament at Belfast represents a considerable devolution of power, but nevertheless great importance is attached to her representation at Westminster, where much of major concern to Northern Ireland is debated and decided.

The Guide, interestingly, also upheld Northern Ireland's freedom to 'take her own decisions at any time' including, by implication, secession from the Union to join what was by then known as Eire. Paradoxically, however, whenever it was suggested that this federal-type relationship might be extended to Scotland, Wales and – most radically of all – to parts of England, the Ulster precedent was pushed from Tory minds and replaced with premonitions of constitutional catastrophe.

As noted above, the federal ideal proved more fertile in an international, or more accurately Imperial, context. The Federal Union movement – which exists to this day in UK and European form – rather quixotically desired global federalism, a sort of federal United Nations, although in the context of the UK's post-war decolonisation, federalism has at best a mixed record. The Caribbean Federation contrived in the mid-1950s lasted barely four years, dissolved in 1962 and was quickly followed by the independence of Jamaica and Trinidad, while the Central African Federation fared little better. The Malaysian Federation, born in September 1962, proved more successful, surviving the early departure of Singapore and the exclusion of

Brunei (landlocked by two Malaysian states), enduring to this day, although not without other political problems.

As John Kendle concluded, the British – by which he meant Foreign and Colonial Office officials – 'generally knew very little about federalism'. 'They accepted that it had its uses for the solution of complex colonial problems,' he reflected, 'but they saw little need to indulge in philosophical reflection about its use.' Again, this was fair comment, and there was an implicit view that what was acceptable in faraway lands of which most British people knew little was not necessarily desirable at home. This was particularly true of the Federal Republic of West Germany, which the UK helped establish in 1949 using territories and frontiers that broadly coincided with those of old Medieval East Francia and the 19th-century Napoleonic Confederation of the Rhine. Although forged in the peculiarly difficult context of post-war Europe, the model proved particularly enduring, strong enough even to absorb East Germany – the old German Democratic Republic – upon reunification in 1990. But then as long as the British 'were playing with other people's sovereignty and not their own, the federal idea held little fear for them,' wrote Kendle, again judiciously. 'Once their own sovereignty was affected, the reaction would be very different.'

He was referring, of course, to devolution at home and moves towards a federal Europe, of which more anon. With decolonisation in full swing (spearheaded, for a period, by the Anglo-Scottish Iain MacLeod) abroad and Nationalist breakthroughs (Plaid Cymru in Wales and the SNP in Scotland) at home, federalism again surfaced as a proposed means of putting the UK's constitutional house in order. Contrary to contemporary rhetoric, however, the then Liberal Party had not been advocating federalism since the age of Gladstone. For a while it had posited 'Home Rule All Round' and then nothing in particular for several decades; only in 1968 did the then Liberal leader Jeremy Thorpe, clearly in response to Plaid and SNP advances, reintroduce the 'federal' idea to his colleagues in the House of Commons on 21 February 1968, calling for parliaments in Scotland and Wales to complement that in Northern Ireland and for a Royal Commission to explore the possibility of 'regional' parliaments in England.

Thorpe said his Bill had two objectives, to involve 'the maximum number of people in the country in decision-taking' and 'to relieve the pressure on Parliament', the latter rationale harking back to previous justifications for Home Rule All Round. Typically, the Liberal leader sought historical provenance for his constitutional pitch, quoting Gladstone in 1879:

I propose that a measure of home rule should be conferred upon different portions of the United Kingdom in order to relieve

Parliament of overwhelming business... If arrangements could be made under which Ireland, Scotland, Wales and portions of England could deal with questions of local and special interest to themselves, that would be the attainment of a great national good.

'If those words were true then,' reasoned Thorpe, 'I suggest that they are even truer now.' But time and again in the UK's constitutional history, he continued, 'we have belatedly conceded in bitterness what could and should have been granted in logic'. Thorpe continued:

If the House concedes that there is a strong case for Parliaments in Northern Ireland, Scotland and Wales, it is logical to ask: what provision should be made in England? It is true that much of England – I am thinking of regions such as the North-East and, indeed, my own area, the South-West – feel as remote from London as do Scotland and Wales. If Wales and Scotland are to have their own Parliaments, it follows that there will remain issues of exclusively English significance. There is clearly a need for a wide measure of devolution. The regions of England are not in the same way the homes of nations, and it is not therefore surprising that there has not yet been great pressure for an English Parliament. Certainly, to take the two Commonwealth examples of Australia and Canada, provincial Legislatures are not unknown.

In short, Thorpe proposed that 'a Federal Parliament would continue to deal with matters such as Foreign Affairs and Defence for the United Kingdom as a whole, and that Parliaments in Wales, Scotland and Northern Ireland would have sole control over their own domestic affairs... and that Members from all parts of the United Kingdom would continue to sit in a Federal Parliament whose total membership could probably be halved'.

This was followed up two months later with a Liberal publication called – in language that would jar today – *Power to the Provinces*. The Scottish Liberal MP David Steel later emerged as an articulate proponent of the federal idea, but prior to 1974 his party was a minority electoral interest – indeed it seemed on the edge of parliamentary extinction for much of the immediate post-war period – and therefore its constitutional thinking held little sway. Instead Steel, Russell Johnston *et al* (sensibly) channelled their energies towards achieving devolution for Scotland and Wales rather than 'all round'.

In any case there was, by the late 1960s, a general clamour for ad hoc rather than holistic constitutional reform. The Labour Prime Minister Harold Wilson had appointed a Royal Commission on the Constitution in 1969, although again this was more a response to Nationalist by-election gains than the manifestation of a genuine desire for UK-wide changes to the machinery of government. Although a cogently-argued minority report eventually recommended something akin to 'devolution all round' (it was at this point that talk of 'Home Rule' fell out of fashion), the main report – published in late 1973 – was dismissive, noting 'very little demand for federalism in Scotland and Wales, and practically none at all in England'. The Commissioners explained:

> It might appear from this description that a federal system would give the individual countries of the United Kingdom a large measure of autonomy. In many important domestic matters they would have sovereign powers which could not be overridden by the central government. Their entrenched position in the constitution would give them a status and influence which the central government would be bound to take into account. At the same time they could still work together in those domestic matters requiring a common policy, and would still form a single state in the eyes of the world.

If this appeared to be approaching approval, it was quickly followed by the conclusion that in practice it 'would not bring the advantages which it might appear to offer in theory'. Typically, the Commissioners caricatured federalism as rigid and inflexible, concluding snootily that it would be 'particularly unsuitable for adoption in the United Kingdom'. The report contained much talk of the 'sovereignty' of Parliament, demonstrating that the political classes were still in thrall to Dicey half a century after his passing.

Federalism, noted the Royal Commission, would be 'foreign to our own tradition of unitary government'. 'We believe', it added, 'that to most people a federal system would appear strange and artificial. It would not provide continuity with the past or sufficient flexibility for the future, and it is unlikely that it would be generally acceptable.' 'In short,' concluded the Commissioners a little more open-mindedly, 'the United Kingdom is not an appropriate place for federalism and now is not an appropriate time.'

But even in the year the Royal Commission reported there were big constitutional changes afoot, and they both involved the ceding, tacitly or otherwise, of such jealously guarded 'sovereignty'. In Northern Ireland a 'border poll' or referendum (a constitutional first in the UK) effectively conceded that the people of the Province were sovereign rather than Parliament, inviting them to choose between membership of the UK and Irish Republic, while in early 1973 the UK had finally joined the then European Economic Community, pooling a degree of sovereignty to Brussels, although naturally this aspect was played down to the electorate, upon entry and again in 1975 when there was a UK-wide referendum on renewed terms of membership.

Events in both Northern Ireland and Brussels demonstrated that old constitutional assumptions were finally breaking down, although not necessarily in a manner conducive to federal ideas being taken more seriously. In the context of Europe, federalism soon came to be associated with excessive *centralisation* rather than decentralisation, while the Province also came under 'direct rule' for the first time since the early 1920s with the abolition of the proto-federal Stormont parliament, thus making the UK more centralised than ever before.

Harold Wilson, Prime Minister again after 1974, went out of his way to rubbish the idea of a federal UK, warning it would mean the insertion of 'judicial determination, theologising, legalistically-inspired findings... into the whole of our economic and social life'. At best it would be 'totally contrived and artificial and at worst unworkable and unwanted'. But as with the Royal Commission's earlier commentary, such a critique hinged upon a caricature of federal governance not to mention a belief that the UK had somehow achieved the most perfect form of government, a smug complacency which, like that in the United States, proved remarkably resistant to empirical evidence. Even relatively modest proposals for devolution unnerved certain members of the Cabinet. When, in 1976, the Labour government finally committed to assemblies for Scotland and Wales, the left-wing firebrand Barbara Castle was horrified, confiding in her diary that the logical end point was 'PR, a written constitution and a Bill of Rights'. Quite why a self-confessed socialist was so concerned about these constitutional innovations was not clear.

There were of course other voices, mainly those of Nationalists, who spoke of pan-UK supranational structures continuing even if Scotland and Wales opted for independence, a so-called 'Council of the Isles'. Yet even the young Alex Salmond, writing in his student newspaper in 1976, lampooned Liberals for believing 'in a federal Scotland, in a federal Britain, in a federal Europe, no doubt in a federal world'. Such cynicism was widespread, even among more radical constitutional agitators.

And although journals such as the *Scotsman* newspaper supported a federal solution to the Scottish and Welsh Questions, as did Lord Hailsham (a past and future Conservative Lord Chancellor), and even

Wilson's government floated proposals for English regional government (largely to balance out its ill-fated proposals for assemblies in Cardiff and Edinburgh), federalism slipped from the agenda, the death knell being further referendums in Scotland and Wales as the 1970s drew to a close. Only the Federal Trust, an offshoot of the Federal Union, explored the issue in a paper published in 1980 but by then, of course, even the devolutionary ship had sailed.

Throughout the 1980s and 1990s demand for devolution grew, and although Liberal Democrats such as Robert Maclennan made valiant efforts to nudge (New) Labour in a more federal, or at least holistic, constitutional direction, John Kendle ended his 1997 book on British federalism on a gloomy note, bemoaning that the UK lacked 'a tradition of open-ended public discussion of constitutional variables'. But after the landslide Labour election victory of 1997 events moved relatively quickly, and within three years (proof that constitutional reform, as in the case of the House of Lords, need not move at a snail's pace) devolution had been restored in Northern Ireland and extended to Scotland, Wales and even London (admittedly in a very weak form). The basis of the UK as a quasi-federal state was set, and the Deputy Prime Minister John Prescott ploughed a lonely furrow on English regionalism, the ill-fated denouement of which came in 2004 when voters in the North East of England rejected a weak form of devolution by a margin of almost four-to-one.

The failure of that ballot stymied talk of rolling out devolution across the UK's largest 'Home Nation' (England, that is) and therefore any prospect of a federal UK or, at the very least, devolution all round. Yet at the same time the Labour governments of Tony Blair (no fan of devolution) had done more than any other since the 1920s to seriously rethink the UK constitution. Indeed, in a 2010 publication called *A Federal Future for the UK: The Options*, Dr Andrew Blick and Professor George Jones suggested 'a broad process of federalisation, rather than the immediate adoption of a federal constitution, has been occurring in the UK'. Many of the reforms initiated between 1997 and 2010 'though not avowedly part of a federal agenda' had nevertheless 'shifted the UK in a federal direction'.

And in doing so, the Labour Party (chiefly responsible for those reforms) had, perhaps unwittingly, opened up previously closed minds; as David Melding wrote in his e-book *A Reformed Union*, constitutional change 'expands the political imagination'. But at the same time federalism still remained the 'f' word in many quarters, something established politicians feared uttering lest it make them appear eccentric or, even worse, like aspirant Liberal Democrats.

CHAPTER 2

Scotland in a Federal UK

[A] system of government in which central and regional authorities are linked in an interdependent political relationship, in which powers and functions are distributed to achieve a substantial degree of autonomy and integrity in the regional units. In theory, a federal system seeks to maintain a balance such that neither level of government becomes sufficiently dominant to dictate the decision of the other, unlike in a unitary system, in which the central authorities hold primacy to the extent even of redesigning or abolishing regional and local units of government at will.

New Fontana Dictionary of Modern Thought

Modern experience suggests several possibilities, none of them congenial to Dicey: that national minorities may be reconciled by a genuine reconstitution of the state into a federation; that such reconstitutions may be accomplished without either weakening the power of the state to make its writ run at home or weakening the nation's power relative to other nations; that federations are not, by the fact of being federations, weaker diplomatically, economically or militarily than unitary states...

Ferdinand Mount, *The British Constitution Now*

The conclusion is simple. Lopsided decentralisation within what purports to be a unitary state will lead to... the disintegration of the United Kingdom. A carefully worked scheme of federation, on the other hand, is likely to make governance more effective and more accountable to its various publics; it will foster the practice of democracy and meet that sense which most people have of showing a number of different identities.   John Barnes, *Federal Britain: No Longer Unthinkable?*

Where should power reside? How is power shared? How are the institutions of government best shaped to deal with the huge challenges of a complex world? How can we best make sure that individuals and communities get the freedoms to control the circumstances of their own lives for the benefit of themselves, their families and their communities?

Scottish Liberal Democrats, *Federalism: The Best Future for Scotland*

ALTHOUGH THE UNITED KINGDOM as currently constituted might possess federal features and, to an outside observer from the United States or Australia, might already look like a *de facto* federation, in a formal sense it is not. As touched upon at the end of Chapter 1, the term that best captures it is *quasi* federal, which still falls short of the definition offered above. Speaking generally, in order to become a proper federation the UK would need an equal distribution of devolution, a formal (codified) statement of the division of powers and a balancing, geographically constituted Upper House of Parliament.

The concept of 'sovereignty' is in this respect important, although frequently overstated. Whereas under a devolved system of government such as that in the UK or Spain power is divested from a central, sovereign authority, under a federal system sovereignty is shared (for example in the United States sovereignty operates in 'parallel' between the federal government, 50 states and American Indian communities).

Therefore *Scotland's Parliament*, the UK government White Paper that set out plans for devolution in 1997, asserts that the 'United Kingdom is and will remain sovereign in all matters', although as I argue below that was more theoretical than real. Similarly, until the Good Friday Agreement of 1998 articles two and three of the Irish constitution asserted sovereignty over Northern Ireland, which of course in practice had been meaningless. As the Conservative constitutionalist Ferdinand Mount argued in his 1992 book *The British Constitution Now*, one must be 'wary of that sleight of hand which bundles together all the attributes of national power and independence and then labels them "sovereignty".' It is not, in short, terribly helpful.

Federalism Liberal Democrat-style

As noted in the previous chapter, since the late 1960s the main proponents of a federal UK have been the Liberals (more recently the Liberal Democrats). Various publications have explored this but most recently Lord Steel (a former Liberal Party leader) restated the party's commitment to a UK federation in his 2005 commission's report *Moving to Federalism – A New Settlement for Scotland*, while another inquiry chaired by Sir Menzies Campbell (a former Liberal Democrat leader) published *Federalism: The Best Future for Scotland* shortly after David Cameron and Alex Salmond signed the Edinburgh Agreement in October 2012.

This called on Scottish Liberal Democrats to 'reassert' their federalist beliefs 'in favour of home rule for Scotland within a reformed, federal UK' while recognising that other parts of the UK might 'wish to move at different speeds'. For the purposes of this short book, this report is a good place to start. Although the Scottish Liberal Democrats, via the Scottish Constitutional Convention and wider devolution debates of the 1980s and '90s, helped 'deliver' the Scottish Parliament, in *Federalism* they claim to have 'always recognised' that devolution 'would only ever be a halfway house to a more permanent modern constitutional framework'. Indeed even ad hoc devolution, the creation of devolved assemblies in Cardiff, London and Belfast, has ended up permanently changing 'the UK constitutional picture'.

Inevitably, federalism involves a defence of, to put it crudely, 'the Union', or certainly aspects of it, but considering that the modern case for independence also involves a continuing role for certain unions (currency, energy, etc), then this is hardly a deal-breaker in terms of attracting broad support. The days of fundamentalist Nationalism (or indeed Unionism) are long gone and pragmatism is the driving force of any new constitutional settlement. The 2006 Steel Commission puts it thus:

> The United Kingdom as a whole has a greater punch internationally than any of its constituent parts separately; the United Kingdom as a whole has financial resources that can be directed to areas of need across Britain; the ability of the United Kingdom to make common provision across the UK for pensions and social security benefits acts as an automatic support for those in greatest need, bringing the resources of the Union to bear in a way which supports areas of greatest economic and social need.

And, as the later *Federalism* report goes on to argue, the 'purpose of the reformed United Kingdom should be to provide a strong and sustainable basis on which to tackle the unprecedented challenges of our age'. It continues:

> Scotland is not and should not be merely another small state on the periphery of Europe, lacking influence in the world. As part of the United Kingdom, Scotland has played a major part in the world. A federal partnership between Scotland and the rest of United Kingdom will further stimulate innovation and energy and be a robust basis on which to deal with the problems of our age.

The Liberal Democrat case for federalism, therefore, can be summarised as follows:

- It gives real democratic choice to the voters of each of the four jurisdictions to decide, within a broad fiscal pact, the nature and extent of public services and how they are delivered. This is particularly important to the people of Scotland at present, but pressure is growing in Wales and Northern Ireland for the greater autonomy of action that would flow from home rule in a federal system.

- It retains the many advantages of the United Kingdom: in fiscal terms; in its single market in capital, labour, enterprise and services; in the operation of some public services at a federal level; and at an international level.
- It retains the ability to deploy the resources of the whole of the United Kingdom to tackle poverty, not least through a UK-wide system of pensions and benefits.
- Unlike the current devolution arrangements, or the centralised system in place before 1999, a federal system would be a permanent and stable solution. It would stand the test of time and contains natural checks and balances that are missing from the UK's current constitutional arrangements.
- It solves the West Lothian Question by creating a system that allows local public policy choices in each jurisdiction to be made autonomously by those elected in that jurisdiction. This remains a major concern amongst English MPs and one that must be addressed in the interest of the stability of the United Kingdom as a whole.

So under a federal settlement, the UK Parliament would concern itself with 'federal matters' (currently known as 'reserved matters') while the Scottish Parliament (and its equivalents in Wales, Northern Ireland, London and – of which more anon – England) would deal with 'Home Rule matters' (currently known as 'devolved matters'). The UK Parliament would therefore be unable to legislate in areas designated competencies of the Home Rule legislatures and, importantly, the division of power and responsibilities between the federal and Home Rule layers of government would be unambiguously codified, unlike at present, of which more below.

The 2009 Calman Commission, although not overly concerned with federalism, set out the division quite clearly:

In a federal system there are (at least) two constitutionally established levels of government. There is at least one function where each level has exclusive competence, and each level is constitutionally free to exercise its competence without the consent of the other level (and, at the lower level, independently of the other states, regions or provinces). In most federations the same structure applies across the territory of the federation, and the governments at each level are accountable to the relevant electorates (i.e. regional or federal).

A formal UK federation (in the eyes of the Liberal Democrats) would also – although arguably this is not strictly necessary – involve further transfer of powers to the Scottish Parliament in Edinburgh. As *Federalism* puts it:

> More devolution alone will not do the job. More devolution will not be the stable long-term solution that our country needs. Constant fiddling with the balance of power and responsibilities does not bring stability. The best solution for Scotland is to combine the existing wide-ranging policy and legislative responsibilities of the Scottish Parliament with substantial revenue-raising powers, all set within the structure of a reformed United Kingdom where the home rule powers are respected and entrenched. That solution is a federal United Kingdom.

But, at the same time, 'the United Kingdom is a union of nations and the people of Scotland cannot change the terms of that union alone'. Scotland, in other words, 'cannot unilaterally impose federalism on the rest of the UK', rather it 'requires the consent and co-operation of the people of England, Wales and Northern Ireland'. This is a pretty fundamental point which federalists would do well to acknowledge; it is also considered more fully below and in the following chapter.

Federalism (Welsh) Conservative-style

UK federalism has not only been advocated by the Liberal Democrats but also, rather eloquently, by David Melding, a Conservative Member of the National Assembly for Wales (and its Deputy Presiding Officer); his various writings on the subject not only compliment proposals from the Scottish Liberal Democrats but flesh them out in several important respects.

As Melding observed in his Institute of Welsh Affairs book, *Will Britain Survive Beyond 2020?* (published in 2009, further evidence that such proposals precede the current referendum debate), a 'great but dormant truth is reasserting itself', that the four UK 'Home Nations' are 'sovereign entities'. Therefore that reality (an unforeseen consequence of the 1999-2000 devolution settlement), Melding argues, has to be recognised in any federal settlement. This was a response to a legitimate point made by many supporters of independence in Scotland and Wales, that in a legal and constitutional sense the Westminster Parliament remained absolutely 'sovereign' and could, in theory if not in practice, over-rule any of the UK's devolved legislatures. In extreme circumstances, the Nationalist argument ran, it might even attempt to extinguish one altogether; after all, that is what the UK government – albeit in exceptional circumstances – opted to do with Northern Ireland's Stormont parliament in 1972.

Scottish, Welsh, Northern Irish and English sovereignty – which already exist in practice if not in constitutional theory – would thus be explicitly recognised, nay guaranteed, within a federal UK. Here Melding finds himself in agreement with the Liberal Democrats and former Labour Prime Minister Gordon Brown, who have both argued for the Scottish Parliament (and by extension the UK's other devolved institutions) to be given *permanence* under a codified constitution or, in Brown's language, a Bill of Rights-type document.

Melding, however, goes further, arguing that 'the fiction of absolute parliamentary sovereignty would end and be replaced by sovereignty over only those areas set out in the constitution' while each Home Nation would also have 'a constitutionally enshrined right to secede' from a UK federation. Although that sounds radical (and indeed such a right certainly does not exist in the United States), it actually formalises a reality implicitly ceded by the 1973 'border poll' in Northern Ireland (which gave the province the option of joining the Irish Republic) and the 2014 Scottish independence referendum.

The strength of Melding's federalist case also lies in its theoretical (he cites, among others, Edmund Burke) and historical depth. 'The Union', he writes in *Will Britain Survive?*, 'is an adventure not a pre-existing entity that was revealed in stages in 1536, 1707, 1801 and 1921. It survives by being modified and re-affirmed by each succeeding generation.' To that list of dates one might add 2014 and, thereafter, the creation of a genuine UK federation. He rightly argues that the 'first step' towards a reformed, federal UK has already been taken by devolving power to Scotland, Wales and Northern Ireland and thus if 'we are to come to terms with federalism' it will 'be necessary to do so thoroughly' by establishing further legislatures in, 'say, Liverpool, Manchester, Birmingham, Newcastle, Norwich and Bristol, Exeter or Southampton', of which more below.

More widely, Melding's 2009 proposals for a federal UK envisage:

- A federal UK Parliament retaining control over 'macro-economic policy, most taxation, immigration and citizenship, defence, and foreign affairs'.

- Sovereignty over 'domestic issues' (including health, education, economic development, transport, housing and planning) would lie with national parliaments in Wales, England, Scotland and Northern Ireland.
- 'It is possible, but initially unlikely, that England might be divided into several units. The federation might also include the crown dependencies of the Isle of Man and the Channel Islands.'
- Westminster would remain a bicameral parliament, but with a smaller House of Commons of 'perhaps 300 MPs' while the House of Lords (or Senators?) 'could be structured to reflect the federation's multinational character', giving each Home Nation 15 out of 100 members to 'promote the principle of equality between the federation's member nations' (Melding later suggested a total of 250 members with a minimum of 30 for each Home Nation).
- A written constitution setting out 'the formal division of sovereignty and the respective rights and responsibilities of the federal and national governments'.
- Any problems or disputes 'would be settled by a Constitutional Court' and the position of the Queen and her successors as Head of State 'would be unchanged'.

It should be pointed out that Melding's thinking on tax (control over which he envisaged being retained at the federal level) had changed by the time he published *The Reformed Union: The UK as a Federation* (also the Institute of Welsh Affairs) as an e-book in late 2013, instead advocating a large degree of fiscal autonomy and therefore 'tax competition' (of which more in Chapter 5).

By 2013, Melding also saw his geographically reconstituted House of Lords (something supported by UKIP's Nigel Farage) giving 'voice to each home nation in influencing and scrutinising state matters such as defence, foreign affairs, and the operation of the British constitution'. Although suspicious of written constitutions, in an April 2014 essay for the *London Review of Books*, the historian Colin Kidd also suggested that the Upper House might be reformed to resemble a 'German-style Bundesrat', reasoning that

with a membership drawn from the governments of the nations and regions of the United Kingdom, the Parliament Acts of 1911 and 1949 repealed, and a supermajority threshold introduced, then the powers of what is effectively England's House of Commons might at last be clipped by a reinvigorated second chamber... It's by no means a panacea, but a new British Bundesrat suggests a modest corrective to the 'democratic deficit' which threatens to push a reluctant Scotland... out of a union which, three centuries after its passage, remains largely unacknowledged in our constitution.

When, early last century, a Conservative backbencher defended the Upper House as the 'watchdog of the constitution', David Lloyd George quipped that it was in fact 'Mr Balfour's poodle' (Arthur Balfour being Conservative leader in the House of Commons at the time), but in a truly federal UK not only might the House of Lords be finally reformed (another old and oft-thwarted dream) but, under the Melding and Kidd plans, might become that constitutional watchdog.

A *written constitution*

Also being watched, and no doubt endlessly interpreted and reinterpreted, would be a new written constitution for the UK, for there is no functioning federation in the world which lacks such a document. It is not strictly true, of course, to say that the UK at present lacks a 'written constitution', for it is certainly *written* down in various documents, for example the Scotland and Wales Acts of 1997 (and their subsequent amendments), but there does not exist a single codified document setting out the division of powers in any formal sense.

In international terms only the UK, New Zealand and Israel do not have a codified constitution, so a federal UK would simply be joining the constitutional mainstream. But for some reason the prospect of a codified constitution – much like discussion of federalism more generally – fills supporters of the status quo with horror. Now it almost goes without saying that codified constitutions are not panaceas (the US version, for example, checks and balances a lot of policies – good and bad – almost to destruction) but at the same time setting out the rules of the game, particularly in constitutional terrain as complicated as the UK's, arguably has merit. As already outlined, most of the rules are already there, they just need gathered together.

As David Melding has written, there will 'come a point when it will be possible to declare that the United Kingdom is a federal union'. 'It would be natural to follow that declaration', he added, 'by a process to produce a comprehensive written constitution for a federal United Kingdom, as is normal across the world.' The Scottish Liberal Democrats agree, arguing that a 'Declaration of Federal Union' might even be 'more significant' than drafting a federal constitution, although such a document 'would be enhanced' by something 'that spoke eloquently of the purposes and principles of the United Kingdom, which was timeless and well-expressed and which would be seen as inspirational'. Hopefully, such a statement would steer clear of hyperbole, but the Lib Dems have a point.

Gordon Brown, the former Labour Prime Minister, has also recently become a convert to a codified constitution, or at least something very like it, talking in a 2014 speech of burying 'for good the idea that Westminster enjoys undivided sovereignty over the country' (similarly Carwyn Jones, the First Minister of Wales, has spoken of 'putting in place a constitution where it is understood what the different levels of government do'. If that meant the 'end of Parliamentary sovereignty', he added, then 'I'm afraid it does'). Brown went on to argue for a clear and codified 'division of powers' between Westminster and a devolved Scotland, a new 'constitutional law' confirming that certain major policy areas ought to remain under UK control as well as the well-being of 'all four nations'. Much of this was echoed in Scottish Labour's *Powers for a Purpose* report on devolution published in March 2014 (although that – like Brown's speech – appeared to think entrenchment of the Scottish Parliament and a formal division of powers was possible *without* a codified constitution).

Precisely what would be included in a UK constitution or federal declaration would of course be subject to as wide a discussion as possible, and not one involving simply the usual suspects, the great and the good as prevalent in Scotland as the rest of the UK. There are several precedents in this respect, in Australia and closer to home in Ireland, both of which made a point of engaging beyond their respective political bubbles. In the context of the written constitution it argues would be required in an independent Scotland, the Scottish Government (or the SNP) has given the unfortunate impression that everything from a ban on nuclear weapons to a right to be housed would be incorporated. Not only does this conflate policy objectives with constitutional aims, but it would leave future governments wide open to legal challenges; constitutions inevitably touch on elements of policy, but the aim ought to be to keep such overlap to a minimum.

A constitution, of course, would require arbitration above and beyond the federal UK parliament. In most federations, most famously in the United States, a 'supreme' or constitutional court fills this role, but while the UK has had its own Supreme Court since 2009, its remit is rather different. It does, however, have a constitutional function even as currently constituted.

Initially the Judicial Committee of the Privy Council, a curious hangover from the colonial era, officiated in 'devolution issues' arising from the Blair-era constitutional reforms, that is questions relating to the powers and functions of the legislatures and governments established in Scotland and Northern Ireland by the Scotland and Northern Ireland Acts of 1998, and questions as to the competence and functions of the legislature and executive established by the Government of Wales Act of 2006.

Under the Constitutional Reform Act of 2005 this function was transferred from the Judicial Committee (which still acts as a final court of appeal for several ostensibly autonomous states as well as the UK's Overseas Territories and Crown Dependencies) to the UK Supreme Court, which can be asked to scrutinise Bills of the Scottish Parliament (under section 33 of the Scotland Act), of the Northern Ireland Assembly (under section 11 of the Northern Ireland Act) and proposed Assembly Bills under section 112 of the Government of Wales Act.

Only one such dispute between the UK Government and a devolved government has actually been taken to the Supreme Court. Nevertheless, disputes are possible if not likely within a formal federation and thus, as the Scottish Liberal Democrats recommend, the Supreme Court (which would undoubtedly need reconstitution) would likely 'exercise jurisdiction in relation to dispute resolution, whilst maintaining that it is not the role of the court to determine substantive political disputes'.

The English Question

England, of course, is the elephant in the federalist room. Shall it have its own pan-English assembly/parliament or a series of smaller, regional legislatures? This is, to say the least, a tricky component of any federalist case and proponents ought to be honest in admitting as much. Melding, usefully, is up front about that, while the Scottish Liberal Democrats have acknowledged that certain parts of a federal UK might proceed at a different pace. In *Will Britain Survive?* Melding acknowledges that 'partial federation' might see Westminster operating in 'two distinct modes', one for English affairs (in which only English MPs would participate), and the other for UK matters. 'This would create an English legislative process *within* Westminster', he writes, 'rather than in a separate English Parliament.' The logic of the recent McKay Commission – charged by David Cameron with answering the West Lothian Question – points to something very like what Melding describes.

As Melding has also argued, federalism offers the opportunity of presenting a more positive justification for an English parliament or *parliaments,* for a UK federation could not hope to survive for very long without having addressed that point. As it stands, devolution carries the risk that the English will one day be governed by a party they did not vote for (as was the case in Scotland between 1979 and 1997). Technically this happened in 2005 (when the Conservatives polled more votes than Labour but won fewer seats), and also in February 1974 and 1964, but in those pre-devolution days it was more generally accepted that the winner of a UK general election took it all, but if it were to happen again – say in May 2015 – then the likely dynamic would be much less tolerable.

But as with federalism more generally, one must be realistic about how purely English governance is likely to develop in the next few years. Back in 2010 Dr Andrew Blick examined the 'federal options' for England in a paper for the Federal Trust, and much of what he discussed remains pertinent. Obviously he considered a federal UK with England as a 'single component' but concluded that while that would offer 'possible advantages', i.e. greater national coherence, the presence of a clear demarcation, etc, it would also dominate a formal federation to an unsustainable degree (even if London was treated as a separate federal unit), while the 'mere existence of an English executive would represent a challenge to the authority of the UK executive'.

Dr Blick also examined the idea, again a very old one, of splitting England into clearly marked 'regions', noting that had John Prescott's desired outcome been achieved post-2004 then it would have constituted 'a major step in a federal direction for the UK, with the entire population being represented by a tier of governance equivalent to a state within a federal constitution'. However the North East rejected the devolution it was offered, and only London possesses a 'regional' unit of devolved governance, albeit very weak.

Another problem with English regions is deciding precisely where one begins and another ends, which usefully has never been a problem when it comes to Scotland and Wales, with historic borders long fixed. The same also applies to the 'City Region' model, although Blick clearly found this prospect appealing. 'Might city regions', he pondered in his 2010 paper, 'offer a federal approach to the structural tensions in the UK?' He cites a 2006 report called 'State of the English Cities' which defined them as 'enlarged territories from which core urban areas draw people for work and services', a good example being Greater Manchester in the North West of England.

Demarcating city regions would, to say the least, be difficult, as many a reorgnisation of English local government – particularly in the North of England – demonstrates. Another challenge, wrote Dr Blick, would 'be achieving coverage of the whole of England that was satisfactory both methodologically and to the electorates in the territories concerned. Where, for instance, would Cornwall be located? In the Plymouth city region?' Also important is public opinion. 'While it is unlikely that the people of England are going to call for federalism within England any time soon,' pondered David Melding (although discontent with the status quo is certainly growing), 'the possibility' nevertheless needs to be contemplated. 'It would certainly reduce, perhaps to insignificance,' he added, 'the problem of the size of England in a UK Federation if England were to be divided into a dozen or so units', but there needed to be 'sufficient time' given for English political institutions to develop (as in Scotland and Wales).

Like Blick, Melding has concluded that city regions offer the most favourable prospect for such decentralisation, arguing that a 'key moment' might come if the Greater London Assembly (GLA) 'ever seeks substantially greater powers'. 'Other cities and regions (indeed City-Regions) might quickly follow London's example', wrote Melding in *The Reformed Union*, 'and be seen as incipient federal units.' To an extent, these demands have already surfaced, originally during Ken Livingstone's tenure as Mayor of London and more ostentatiously under Boris Johnson's 'city state' agenda. Johnson even charged the London School of Economics' Tony Travers to explore the possibility of fiscal powers for the GLA, and he concluded that the 'practicalities of establishing [a new] Scottish tax regime suggest there are no insuperable obstacles to the devolution of tax powers to any other part of the UK'.

In a major speech delivered in Birmingham in April 2014 the Labour leader Ed Miliband added his voice to the city region debate, promising (should he become Prime Minister in May 2015) 'the biggest economic devolution of power to England's great towns and cities in a hundred years'. Echoing proposals from the former Conservative Deputy Prime Minister Michael Heseltine, Miliband said he would be willing to hand over £4 billion a year of Whitehall expenditure to city and country regions willing to work across present local authority boundaries, the details of which would be drawn up by former Cabinet minister Lord Adonis's 'Growth Review'.

Authorities that brought together plans in the first nine months of a Labour government would, pledged Miliband, receive a devolution deal in time for the first spending review, including new powers over transport and housing infrastructure funding, as well as for the Work Programme and skills training. Adonis was also reporting to be 'looking closely' at the devolution of tax-raising powers to new city regional authorities, and was consulting with Tony Travers, who had recommended devolving similar powers to London's Mayor.

Although all of this sounded bold, it was very much in the groove of the debate as it stood in 2012–14. Indeed, the Cities Minister Greg Clark had already pushed forward so-called 'City Deals' involving similar funding and powers, although most nascent city regions generally argued for going much further. As Lord Heseltine and the IPPR had argued in another context, the North of England – and other English regions – would all benefit from having their own Alex Salmonds to stand up for their respective areas.

However the English Question is eventually answered, its size relative to the rest of the UK is not as big an issue as at first might appear. The United States, for example, has states that range from populations of under 600,000 (Wyoming) to more than 37 million (California). 'Consequently', as Blick and Jones put it in 2010, 'there is no reason a territory such as Cornwall, with a population of around half a million, could not be a single component in a federal UK alongside other larger units', which would presumably include the South East of England (most likely shorn of London).

Nor is uniformity in terms of powers a necessary precondition of a federal UK. Although Spain is not a formal federation, its regions (historic and otherwise) enjoy varying degrees of autonomy – the Basque Country has the closest thing to 'fiscal autonomy' in Europe. The Canadian Provinces do not all possess the same constitutional powers, a consequence of several reforms not to mention repeated concessions to demands from Quebec. So while the English elephant is undoubtedly large it is not immovable.

After all, English 'regions' already exist when it comes to the Barnett Formula, regional development, Local Enterprise Partnerships and so on, just not as strongly in the public consciousness. As has been demonstrated in Wales – which only narrowly backed devolution in the 1997 referendum – initially unloved institutions can bed in over time, and the same would be true in England. A federal UK would help make the case.

How will federalism be achieved?

Now this is all very and good in theory, but politics is, of course, the art of the possible rather than the art of the *theoretically* possible, so how is federalism to be achieved? 'A simple declaration is needed,' writes David Melding in *The Reformed Union*, 'perhaps codified in the first clause of a new Act of Union – that Britain is a federation with each of its parliaments indissoluble and sovereign over their apportioned jurisdiction.'

That is certainly desirable, although arguably far from simple. Not only would such a declaration require considerable political boldness, but it would need to attract a degree of public support in order to reach fruition.

If, however, the former can be achieved then it is highly likely the latter would follow; for reasons discussed earlier, public opinion in each part of the UK is open to persuasion on this front.

Nevertheless turning public opinion in favour of a UK federation would require patience and commitment, just as the long campaign for a Scottish Parliament did in the 1980s and 1990s. Cross-party agreement would also be fundamental, and most protagonists in the independence debate agree that some sort of forum in the wake of the referendum (assuming a 'no' vote) would be desirable. A Royal Commission (as in 1969–73) might be one means of achieving a consensus, although the counter-argument that such bodies 'take minutes and waste years' does give cause for concern. David Melding favours a Speaker's Conference (like that which recommended a federal scheme in the early 1920s) involving the Commons Speaker and the three devolved bodies' Presiding Officers, while the Labour Shadow Cabinet member Douglas Alexander has proposed a 'National Convention' to reach agreement – not just on the constitution – in late 2014.

The Liberal Democrats and Conservatives in Scotland have made positive noises about Alexander's proposal, while Scottish Tory leader Ruth Davidson said 'we must find a means whereby we do not lurch from one commission to another, year after year; where the constitutional and commercial certainty we all crave is never reached'. 'Where devolution is not viewed as a bilateral arrangement between Holyrood and Westminster, Cardiff Bay and Westminster or Stormont and Westminster,' she added, 'but a mechanism which reviews devolution across – and within – our whole United Kingdom.'

On behalf of the Scottish Liberal Democrats, in early 2014 Sir Menzies Campbell set out a 'timetable for action' following a 'no' vote in the referendum, presenting the Calman process and resulting Scotland Act as 'a persuasive example of what can be achieved'. He saw the journey towards a UK federation panning out as follows:

- Provisions in the 2015 Queen's Speech to 'strengthen the powers of Scotland within the United Kingdom'.
- Led by the Scotland Office, the UK Government should analyse the options available to enhance the powers of the Scottish Parliament.
- The Scottish Government should share officials' 'research and knowledge' to inform this process.
- The Scottish Parliament should ensure the independent fiscal body which will support the tax powers in the 2012 Scotland Act is designed to cope with other financial powers should they be devolved following a 'no' vote.

- The Secretary of State for Scotland should convene a meeting within 30 days of the referendum to 'secure a consensus for the further extension of powers to the Scottish Parliament consistent with continued membership of the United Kingdom and to be included in party manifestos for the 2015 general election'.
- Political parties should include commitments in their May 2015 election manifestos.
- The necessary changes should be made through a further Scotland Act, which would also see the 'entrenchment' of the Scottish Parliament via resolutions at Westminster and Holyrood.

This, it has to be said, is rather cautious and is Scotland-centric rather than a more holistic UK approach. Nevertheless it is feasible and mirrors previous constitutional changes. The 'Campbell II' paper (numbered so as to differentiate it from the Lib Dems' original *Federalism* publication, over which Sir Menzies also presided) also identifies a consensus – based on contributions from politicians, think tanks, civic organisations and academics – around two propositions:

- That the Scottish Parliament's financial powers should be expanded so that it is responsible for raising the taxes to pay for the majority of its spending;
- That the Scottish Parliament should be entrenched permanently, in Gordon Brown's word, 'indissoluble'.

These two propositions, noted Campbell II, were 'entirely normal in federal systems around the world'. 'Indeed they represent essential federal characteristics of such systems,' added the report. 'They can be secured for Scotland's relationship with the rest of the UK now, allowing other constituent parts of the United Kingdom to adopt them should they choose to do so.'

These might appear to be baby steps rather than a 'big bang' approach to federal constitutional reform, but then one has to be realistic: constitutional change in the UK, as the Liberal Democrats have correctly noted, 'tends to be incremental and untidy rather than revolutionary'. This, arguably, is a strength, for new arrangements would build on the practice and successes of the past while eliminating the weaknesses; after all, even the much-vaunted US constitution developed over a considerable period of time. As David Melding has engagingly argued, not only would federalism in a UK context have a good chance of achieving political consensus, it would also represent 'an organic development of Britain's parliamentary tradition', gradually working 'towards common ground that could accommodate the most constructive elements of unionist and nationalist thought'. It is quite a thought.

CHAPTER 3

Objections to a Federal UK

ALL OF THIS sounds very tidy, very neat, an almost unanswerable case, but of course no constitutional scheme is ever perfect; even federalism has weaknesses (though I would suggest fewer than independence or ad hoc devolution). Still, in the spirit of open discourse, it is worth identifying what appear to be the principal arguments *against* a federal UK and attempt to deal with them in turn.

England is too big...

David Melding called this the 'Prussian' problem and acknowledged it as 'easily the strongest objection to federalism being adopted in the United Kingdom'. England, of course, is the largest – in terms of population, land mass and economy – of the UK's Home Nations and opponents of federalism argue it would completely dominate a UK federation. This is both a legitimate point and also an overstatement. Although other federations, for instance Canada, have federal units of unequal size (between them Quebec and Ontario have a population of 20 million, nearly twice the population of the other provinces combined), even so a formal federation would diminish the current dominance of England within the UK (which of course has already been reduced, in legislative terms, through devolution), via a formal division of powers, the removal of the West Lothian Question, a geographically balanced House of Lords and a constitutional court to arbitrate in disputes between the four Home Nations. England undoubtedly dominated the old, pre-1999 UK, but less so now, and even less under a federal settlement.

It's never going to happen...

This is an inherently conservative argument. At points in modern UK history universal suffrage, votes for women, a female Prime Minister,

BRITAIN REBOOTED – SCOTLAND IN A FEDERAL UNION

devolution and especially Scottish independence were 'never going to happen' or were at least considered highly unlikely. As Melding argues in *Will Britain Survive?*, those who dismiss federalism as 'fanciful' fail to appreciate that the UK 'has already reached functional federalism and, in a sense, constitutional theory needs to catch up with political practice'. Any first-time visitor to the UK from, say, Canada, the US or Australia, would recognise a UK governed from London at one level and from Edinburgh, Cardiff and Belfast at another as a loosely federal structure of government.

It's a slippery slope...

Unreconstructed Unionists (mainly to be found, curiously, in the Labour Party) sometimes argue, as they did in the 1970s and 1990s, that further constitutional change, particularly federalism, is little more than a 'slippery slope' towards eventual independence for Scotland and perhaps also Wales and Northern Ireland (as a precursor to Irish reunification). Of course that is possible – just think of Yugoslavia – but also true of the status quo. Such an analysis, taken to its logical conclusion, would not recognise difference or variation within the UK in any form and would harmonise three different legal systems, four separate education systems and two 'national' religions for the sake of a strong centre and national cohesiveness. No one, for obvious reasons, is suggesting any such thing. Lots of federal countries – most notably the United States – have not been in danger of breaking up in more than a century, but of course secession would be the democratic choice of each Home Nation; it is difficult to argue that federalism (particularly given the events at time of writing) would make it any more likely.

Federalism is 'alien' to the UK constitutional tradition...

At first glance, this seems a reasonable point to make, but in reality misunderstands both domestic constitutional development and also the UK's imperial legacy. Not only did the British Cabinet seriously consider federalism in the early 1920s (with many Scots among its most ardent proponents), but 'parliamentary federalism' was actually a British invention, initially developed for use in large 'Dominions' such as Australia, Canada and South Africa. Much later, when the British Empire was being dismantled, the Foreign Office drafted dozens of federal constitutions and frameworks for departing colonies (some, admittedly, more successful than others), while in the wake of the Second World War the UK helped fashion one of the world's most successful federations, West Germany.

Federalism would be too complicated and bureaucratic...

This is a bit of a red herring, for only a fully unitary UK would lack any complexity, and the British constitution has moved well beyond that. Of course federalism would complicate – to an extent – the governance of the UK, but then those making that point must acknowledge that the status quo with lop-sided ad hoc devolution and no specific allowance for England is already pretty complicated. Federalism would tidy up the rather convoluted current settlement and, importantly, clarify the rules of the game. Furthermore, simply responding to the demand of a significant minority for independence by pledging to extend the existing powers of the Scottish Parliament risks making the current settlement *even more* complicated.

Federalism would need support from the rest of the UK...

This is of course true, for federalism cannot be imposed on the rest of the UK by Scotland alone (some commentators have argued that 'devo-max' would constitute unilateral federalism, which of course it would not), but there is evidence that a formal federation would find favour in all the Home Nations. Although (to my knowledge) support for federalism has never been formally gauged by a pollster, most surveys do reveal that majority opinion in Scotland and Wales favours more autonomy rather than independence or the status quo. Sure, further ad hoc devolution might satisfy that desire but only federalism does so in a stable, coherent way. Importantly, opinion has also shifted in England, away from general contentment about the UK's uneven distribution of devolved power and towards greater unhappiness with the status quo. Although several surveys demonstrate that English public opinion does not congregate around any single option (for example an English Parliament), it is reasonable to posit that it would hardly be hostile to a UK federation in which the governance of England would be dealt with for the first time since 1999.

Federalism isn't independence...

Indeed it is not, but then nor is the status quo. A federal UK would explicitly preserve certain functions – chiefly defence, foreign affairs and currency – under federal jurisdiction, but then both Unionists and Nationalists now acknowledge that a multi-national state must also enjoy multi-level governance. For the last decade the SNP has been ostentatiously relaxed about a devo-max model for Scotland in which defence and foreign affairs are reserved to the UK Parliament, while more recently it has argued for a 'currency union' governing use of sterling, thus none of this ought to be a deal-breaker for those on the independence end of the spectrum. And even under a formal federation, each of the Home Nations (including, of course, Scotland) would still retain influence, arguably *greater* influence, over those reserved areas, not only through a written constitution but also via a rebalanced House of Lords.

Conclusion

By way of comparison, one might substitute this chapter with a lengthy description of all the shortcomings inherent in the status quo, independence, the pre-1997 model of UK governance, and so on. The point is – as set out at the beginning of this section – all systems of government have pros and cons; federalism is not innately superior, nor is it automatically a bad idea. But, I would contend, the most common objections to federalism have more to do with dogma and constitutional conservatism than any serious, judicious analysis of the facts.

CHAPTER 4

Double Federalism

Local Government is elected; has its own tax; its own powers from Parliament; and is responsible, in distinct areas, for public services from cradle to grave, 24 hours a day, and in emergencies. It is a unique element of our government and Constitution. Since the federal idea values decentralisation, to avoid power being monopolised in one central place, federalists should champion local government.

Professor George Jones, A Federal Future for the UK: The Options

So what if we set those councils free to pursue new opportunities? A basket of taxes to be set locally. Community banking underwritten by the new Scotland Act's borrowing powers and charged with growing businesses out of universities and skilled citizens out of colleges. Curricula in schools tailored locally to help young people into local jobs and industries. Budgets set in communities so citizens can take ownership of the place around them and responsibility for making it better.

Michael Marra, Towards the Local: Devolution and Democratic Renewal in Scotland

I quickly learned that Scotland is also a league of city-states... In American terms, Glasgow is like Chicago and Edinburgh is like Boston; they are as close as Berkeley is to Stanford and just as different from each other.

Professor Richard Rose, Learning About Politics in Time and Space

ALTHOUGH RECOGNITION OF England, Scotland, Northern Ireland and Wales as the UK's four Home Nations would be the central element of any federal Union, the spirit of federalism ought not to end there. There is a growing consensus in Scotland, and indeed across the UK, that local government has over the last few decades lost too much power at the hands of all governments, devolved and central, Labour and Tory, Unionist and Nationalist, thus a federal settlement offers a good opportunity to redress the balance of power *within* Scotland as well as *within* the UK.

This is not an original point. The Scottish Liberal Democrats' 2012 paper, *Federalism: The Best Future for Britain*, pointedly looked beyond central government, and proposed 'extensive autonomy' for local government, including the transfer of power over council and business rates back to councils. Similarly, 'localism' is also a common buzzword among opposition Labour politicians and within the present Conservative-Liberal Democrat Coalition at Westminster. Of course, a cynic would observe that all political parties promise to decentralise while in opposition but do precisely the opposite in office, and that cynic would usually be sadly correct. The incumbent Coalition's Programme for Government, for example, states that it 'will promote the radical devolution of power and greater financial autonomy to local government and community groups', although the actions of Communities Secretary Eric Pickles have often been contrary to that aim. A federal UK, however, arguably offers greater scope for genuine decentralism than the status quo.

As Professor George Jones argues in *A Federal Future for the UK: The Options* (published by the Federal Trust in 2010), local government 'expresses the federal spirit of opposition to the concentration of governmental power in one unitary place'. A federal Act of Union should clearly set out the responsibilities of local authorities and end the treatment of local government as if, to quote George Jones again, 'it were a division of central government'. As with the UK's four Home Nations, its status should be embedded in statute to prevent incessant tinkering from the centre. If the aim of federalism is to govern at the right level, then the same should be true within each of the Home Nations. Although Scotland is small relative to England, it is large enough to encompass diversity befitting constitutional recognition. *As Federalism: The Best Future for Britain* argues, Home Rule for Scotland 'is part of this process but, by itself, insufficient'.

Financing local government

Responsibility for raising money as well as spending it is key, and while local authorities in Scotland and across the UK used to be responsible for the vast majority of what they spent, today only around 15 per cent of local revenue is actually controlled by Scottish councils (the rest coming from a central government grant), a proportion the rolling council tax freeze in Scotland keeps artificially low. Possessing almost no independent revenue-raising mechanism to support the public services they provide is a situation almost unique in a European context.

This immediately puts local government at a disadvantage, giving it – as is the case with the Scottish Parliament as currently constituted – power without responsibility. Thus the status quo positively encourages central (UK or Scottish) government incursions into what ought to be clearly demarcated local responsibilities, while it also limits the choices that can be put before voters by municipal lawmakers. The Scottish Liberal Democrats propose giving local authorities responsibility for raising around half the money they spend locally 'in order to improve accountability and local power'.

Professor George Jones, in his 2010 paper, argued for a similar proportion derived from a mix of (a reformed, 'fairer') property tax and a new Local Income Tax, which of course was Liberal Democrat and SNP policy at the 2007 Scottish Parliament elections. Professor Jones envisaged a situation where 'local government will no longer be dependent for most of its revenue on central government, acting like a drug addict always seeking its fix of central grant'. He ruled out relying on a sales tax or VAT on the basis that neither would 'promote local accountability'.

Therefore the Liberal Democrats are correct to argue that the council tax freeze must end (though it will undoubtedly be politically difficult), with rates and other locally controlled taxes in each council returning to the control of locally-elected councillors, who are of course accountable to their respective electorates. The same goes for business rates, the revenue from which should be retained in its entirety by each local authority.

(As an aside, a reform of local property taxation is long overdue, particularly considering the current – frozen – council tax regime is based upon valuations conducted more than two decades ago. Liberal Democrats talk of a 'mansion tax', but this is probably a red herring; much more desirable would be what the commentator Will Hutton calls 'a wholesale overhaul' with a graduated property tax on all homes above £300,000, adding several bands to take account of regional variations – both within Scotland and the UK – and, more to the point, the vast increase in property prices since the Community Charge, or 'Poll Tax', was abolished in the early 1990s.)

Current local authority expenditure is around £17 billion, about half the Scottish Government's block grant, and under Lib Dem proposals councils would raise about half that amount via council tax, business rates and other fees, charges and specific grants from central government. That is a broadly sensible balance and would be a vast improvement upon the status quo.

Ironically, as well as centralising local government spending (via the council tax freeze), the present Scottish Government has, via an 'historic' (some might say hysterical) concordat with the Convention of Scottish Local Authorities, single outcome agreements and effective nationalisation of fire and police services, substantially weakened the scope for localism within Scotland. Indeed, the SNP's definition of 'localism' appears to regard Scotland as local enough. Reversing certain elements of this (chiefly police and fire services) would likely be costly and bureaucratic, but there is still scope for moving towards much greater decentralisation in a way, as the Lib Dems put it, 'that enhances local accountability and allows communities to choose the solutions and services that suit their needs'.

Local government organisation

Usefully, local government is somewhat tidier in Scotland, Wales and Northern Ireland than it is in England. Scotland currently has 32 local authorities, Wales 22 and Northern Ireland 26, all of them unitary. England, though centrally governed relatively simply, is extremely complex; being subdivided into 48 'counties' with a mix of county, district and parish councils, some unitary and some two-tier (as used to be the case in Scotland), the result of incremental reforms in 1965 and 1974.

In *Federalism: The Best Future for Britain* the Scottish Liberal Democrats argued that there was 'no case for a wholesale reform of local government or the re-establishment of two-tier local government' but concluded there was 'a case for local burgh councils where communities demand change'. The Scottish Greens also find this idea attractive, although it is tinged with nostalgia for the pre-1974 local government map of Scotland with its panoply of small parish, town and county authorities. Conceived by the respected land reform campaigner Andy Wightman, the party wants to 'move towards much smaller units of government that would be able to raise the majority of their funding locally'. The Scottish Greens' proposals include:

- Breaking current councils down into municipalities serving around 20,000 people each (European municipalities, they point out, average 5,600 people).
- A set of larger regions to co-ordinate issues such as health, economic development, colleges and transport.
- A flexible 'Lego brick' model for co-ordinating other services between the smaller units.
- Municipalities should raise at least 50 per cent of their own revenue.
- Local government should get a statutory share of national income tax.
- The status of local government should be enshrined in a written constitution for the first time.

There is much to admire in this 'small is beautiful' programme, and – usefully – there is a degree of overlap with the Scottish Liberal Democrats' own suggested reforms. However, the central idea of moving towards smaller units of local government is unconvincing, particularly when the aim is to encourage greater voter engagement. In truth, this is extremely difficult to do. The move towards electing Scottish local authorities via the Single Transferable Vote, for example, was supposed to increase engagement, accountability and so on, but while turnout (40 per cent) in 2012 was the highest in the UK, it remained markedly below that for Holyrood and Westminster elections (STV did end Labour's stranglehold on Scottish councils, however, which was demonstrably a good thing).

As the Scottish Greens have themselves noted, turnout in local government by-elections is often extremely low (one recent ballot in Govan attracted just 20 per cent). The Scottish Government's experiment with elections to health boards has also been a damp squib, as were directly-elected police and crime commissioners in England and Wales, a US device grafted on to UK politics and an ill-conceived one at that. Similarly, when the Westminster Coalition carried out its pledge to introduce directly elected mayors for the eleven largest English cities, subject to referenda, it was an embarrassing flop, with only two actually voting 'yes', and not exactly with large majorities (to be more precise, Bristol voted for and Doncaster voted to retain its directly-elected mayor).

Politicians, particularly Greens and Liberal Democrats, are guilty of overestimating the desire among voters to have even more elections. Of course a legitimate counter-argument is that the English mayors (as with the 2004 North East Assembly referendum) were not granted, at least not immediately, significant new powers (another Coalition pledge), and thus voters declined to take the offer seriously. Nevertheless, local government reorganisation is notoriously difficult to get right, as the amount of ongoing grumbling about the Scottish reforms of 1975 and 1995 demonstrates, and reformers – particularly federalists – ought to tread carefully.

There is, meanwhile, a credible case to be made for returning to the eight regional authorities that represented the upper tier of Scottish local authorities for two decades between those two previous reforms. Although unpopular with Conservatives (who resented, in particular, Labour dominance of Strathclyde Regional Council), they were actually reasonably effective units of local governance, and indeed their relative size was more often than not an advantage, enabling them to co-ordinate services such as transport, education and planning across larger areas. Indeed, the Scottish Greens hint at this with their proposal for a 'set of larger regions to coordinate issues such as health, economic development, colleges and transport'.

The obvious model is that which existed previously, and indeed did until recently when Scotland's representation in the European Parliament was divided into eight large regional constituencies. In political terms this would be easier to sell to voters than the creation of (potentially) hundreds of *additional* local authorities as per proposals from the Scottish Greens, while the resulting administrative consolidation could help local authorities cut costs.

Regionalism within Scotland

Scotland, it is important to remember, has already been decentralised in several respects, and certainly much more so than in England where London dominates politically, economically and culturally. If anything, Aberdeen and the Aberdeenshire region (formerly Grampian) has long been the economic powerhouse of Scotland and of course its (and the UK's) energy capital; Edinburgh is naturally the political and historical centre while Glasgow, Scotland's largest city, has long been established as Scotland's media and cultural hub.

Even in overly-centralised England, Manchester – and its surrounding region – has demonstrated that it is possible to compete, certainly in economic and cultural terms, with London and the South East. Furthermore, Manchester demonstrates what can be achieved even outwith formal devolution, for it enjoys few of the constitutional advantages possessed by Wales to its west and Scotland to its north. Manchester plotted a course even within the centralised status quo; political will – and political vision – was key.

The renaissance of Manchester was spearheaded by powerful civic leaders (again without huge executive powers), as has also been the case in Birmingham and the West Midlands region. Not only does this strengthen the case for city region-based federalisation of England (as explored in Chapter 2), but perhaps the direct election of Lord Mayors in England and Lord Provosts in Scotland. Only the Scottish Conservatives are currently committed to giving Scots the option of changing the structure of their local authority. As the party's 2012 local government manifesto pledged:

> We would hold referenda in Aberdeen, Glasgow, Dundee and Edinburgh to give people the opportunity to elect a powerful provost. The exact nature of the post would be a matter of consultation and for each council to decide what is most appropriate for their area but we would expect elected provosts to take on powers of current council leaders, some of the Chief Executive, as well as the ceremonial roles of Lord Provosts.

Such a move would help bolster what might be called double federalism, i.e. strong decentralisation not only within the UK and its constituent Home Nations, but also within Scotland. Directly-elected Lord Provosts leading four (out of perhaps a total of eight) powerful city regions might not only lead the economic and cultural revival of Scotland's historic civic centres, but also act as a much needed counterweight against a centralising Scottish Government. Not only would federalism rewrite the rules of the game in UK terms, but the rules of the game within Scotland.

CHAPTER 5

Fiscal Federalism

No self-respecting parliament should expect to exist permanently on 100% hand-outs determined by another parliament, nor should it be responsible for massive public expenditure without any responsibility for raising revenue in a manner accountable to its electorate.

The Steel Commission: Moving to Federalism – A New Settlement for Scotland

Since it came back in 1999 (after 292 years), the parliament has been about doling out, and maximising, its grant from Westminster. It's been easy for it to have strong rhetoric about good things to do on social policy... the political class have been very good at arguing the cases for money for Scotland. They've been less effective about allocating it within Scotland between areas of growth and decline... and they've certainly not often been prepared to think about the budgetary realities of policies that get promised.

Duncan Maclennan, the *Guardian*

A FEDERAL UNITED KINGDOM would, of course, require a means of financing itself. At present, the UK is relatively centralised in terms of tax and spend with the Treasury ruling the roost. The so-called 'Barnett Formula' (actually not a formula at all), meanwhile, governs how public expenditure is distributed between the nations and regions of the UK. This has been the case since the late 1970s and was famously supposed to be a temporary measure, in anticipation of the failed attempt to devolve power to Scotland and Wales in 1979 (and the possible revival of the Northern Ireland Parliament). A devolved parliament cannot simply be about spending money rather than raising it, for that is the power of politics without much responsibility.

Barnett, like so many other features of the present UK constitution, hint at federalism, not just in terms of Scotland, Wales and Northern Ireland but in its treatment of England not as a homogenous whole but as distinct regions. Barnett is also much misunderstood; it distributes, for example, an above-average level of public spending even to London, the wealthiest part of the UK. Scotland arguably benefits while Wales loses out, but just as the direction of travel in constitutional terms points towards an increasingly federal UK, so too do recent fiscal developments.

The Scotland Act of 2012, for example, included several incremental changes in the fiscal powers of the Scottish Parliament due to take effect in 2015/16. That Act, although welcome, had already been overtaken by events when it received Royal Assent, for in the wake of the 2011 Holyrood elections the three Unionist parties began to consider devolving income tax in its entirely rather than just 10p in each band as a result of the Calman Commission's recommendations. This is likely to form the basis of Conservative, Labour and Liberal Democrat manifesto commitments in 2015 and 2016 (although at the time of writing Scottish Labour appears to be having second thoughts). In Wales, meanwhile, the Holtham and Silk proposals both point towards greater fiscal devolution along Scottish lines.

Another product of the 2012 Scotland Act is the Joint Exchequer Committee that, as the Scottish Liberal Democrats have observed, constitute 'necessary mechanisms to the effective functioning of quasi-federal arrangements'. The earlier Steel Commission on federalism used the term 'fiscal federalism' to describe the financial underpinning of the move to a more federal UK, determining the allocation of fiscal responsibilities and powers to different tiers of government across the nations and regions of the UK. Steel explained it thus:

> Fiscal equity is a crucial principle in any federal system. Academics are clear that no industrialised countries have opted for full fiscal autonomy. The reason for this is clear: to do so strikes against the principle of unity within states that sees an element of redistribution between areas with different levels of income and wealth. All federal states include some form of intergovernmental transfers. It forms part of the social pact and in many cases the written legal constitution that binds the constituent parts of the state together. It recognises the benefits to all of the federal union and the need for solidarity.

Fiscal federalism recognises that while it is desirable for the Home Nations – and local authorities within those Home Nations – to raise as much of the money they spend as possible, at the same time a system of fiscal transfers is desirable not just in terms of federal unity but also in order to deliver social justice.

Although the 2009 Calman Commission was rather dismissive about federalism, it did recognise that the Scottish Parliament already enjoyed 'a remarkably high degree of spending freedom and accountability, much greater than that of many state or provincial governments in federal systems in other countries'. The Commissioners also noted that other countries, mostly federations, had chosen to adopt different combinations of funding mechanisms. As the Commission's final report observed, all had developed according to 'the history and the constitutional arrangements and objectives of the countries concerned'.

The same would be true of a federal UK. Indeed, the Calman Commission drew particular inspiration from Canada, whose Provinces are funded 'by a mix of transfers from the federal government, devolved taxation revenues and revenues from taxes shared with the Federal Government'. The principal grants paid to Provinces are designed to achieve certain minimum standards in healthcare, social provision and education and are transferred on a per capita basis to ensure equality of provision. Finally, an equalisation grant also paid to the Provinces is calculated on the basis of equalising fiscal capacity rather than actual need. The Calman Commission envisaged its Scottish Variable Rate – under which 10p in each income tax band will be controlled in Edinburgh as of 2015/16 – as a 'modest example' of the Canadian model, under which different levels of government share the same tax base with a common (usually federal) collection authority, in the UK's case Her Majesty's Revenue and Customs (HMRC).

The Scottish Liberal Democrat *Federalism* report recognised there was a 'strong case' for retaining an integrated UK tax collection system to underpin a federal UK's single capital and labour market, but with the income tax raised by Scots coming under the complete control of Holyrood. This makes a lot of sense and is entirely consistent with other federal systems around the world. So under that system, tax paid at source on personal income from savings and investments would be a federal responsibility, albeit with an estimated share of the Scottish proceeds allocated to the Scottish Parliament (and likewise in the other Home Nations).

In other words, HMRC would apply the tax rates as determined by the Scottish Parliament *et al*, while powers over Capital Gains and Inheritance Tax might be allocated to the Home Nations. On top of Stamp Duty Land Tax (which Calman recommended be devolved to Holyrood), the Scottish Liberal Democrats also want devolved responsibility for the Aggregates Levy and Air Passenger Duty. Obviously agreement over which taxes ought to be federal or state-level will not always be harmonious; more important are the fiscal mechanisms that would finance a UK federation, and by its very nature such a system would have to be highly flexible. In a March 2014 speech the former Labour Prime Minister Gordon Brown argued for a formal 'tax-sharing agreement' to set out which spending areas would remain under Westminster control and those controlled by the devolved governments, which sounded very much like the financial basis of a UK federation.

Tax competition?

Corporation Tax may loom large in the context of the Scottish independence debate but in many respects it is a red herring, for few companies pay all of what will soon be a 20 per cent rate (indeed, Ireland illustrates the sizeable gap between headline and actual rates of corporate taxation paid). The SNP leader Alex Salmond has made much of undercutting the UK rate by 3 per cent (no matter, it seems, how low the Treasury goes), something he believes would give an independent Scotland a competitive advantage, although given that just across the Irish Sea the headline rate is almost five points lower than that (12.5 per cent), this is difficult to take seriously.

There are also legitimate concerns that devolving Corporation Tax to the Scottish Parliament (the Northern Ireland Assembly has led the charge in demanding this, a Westminster response to which is due after the referendum for obvious reasons) and, by logical extension, to the other Home Nations, that a race to the bottom will ensue. As David Melding argued in his recent book:

> There is a tendency for jurisdictions to compete against each other for mobile economic resources. In making the provision of public services more efficient, this competition is productive. However, the balance is a fine one and beggar-thy-neighbour tax policies result in a race to the bottom where tax rates are set too low to generate an optimum level of public goods and services.

For similar reasons, the Scottish Liberal Democrat *Federalism* commission was 'concerned that variable rates or regimes for Corporation Tax across the United Kingdom could encourage businesses simply to switch their registered offices between jurisdictions to no overall economic benefit'. Instead it recommended *assigning* the estimated Scottish proceeds of Corporation Tax to the Scottish Parliament. Oil and gas revenues were also examined by the Lib Dems, who concluded that these were best dealt with federally, although with the belated establishment of an oil investment fund *à la* Norway, but only once there was a fiscal surplus (in which case this is best viewed as a long-term commitment), 'allocating the proceeds to the benefit of Scotland, England, Wales and Northern Ireland on federal principles'. This seems a sensible compromise, but then Liberal Democrats are good at coming up with sensible compromises. (For those unduly concerned, meanwhile, about a 'race to the bottom' in fiscal terms, the point was surely ceded back in 1999 when the Scottish Parliament was equipped with tax-varying powers, however academic, a function extended by another Scotland Act in 2012 and soon to be echoed in Wales.)

Taken together, devolved and assigned taxation under the Lib Dem model would account for the majority of Scottish Government spending, with the balance funded by an equalising payment from the UK Treasury, a perfectly standard feature of other federal systems and, of course, mirrored by the present Barnett system. As *Federalism* concludes:

> The recommendations on tax strike two balances. They balance equity across the United Kingdom with the desire for greater decision-making powers and incentives for the Scottish Parliament. And they balance the freedom to adopt different taxation policies in different parts of the UK against the need to minimise the risks of tax avoidance by those with the wealth to exploit such differences.

Under a federal UK this balance of tax and spend would of course change over time, but the beauty of it is that not only would the Home Nations be able to create completely new taxes (an ability that will already exist post-2015/16), but what Alex Salmond calls the 'social union' would continue to be underpinned by a federal layer of collection and expenditure mainly addressing respective need in the nations and regions of the UK.

So the Barnett Formula, the death of which has often been predicted, need not necessarily disappear under UK fiscal federalism; it could even remain – in modified form – to provide balancing payments to different parts of the UK. The Liberal Democrats, however, have long believed it ought to be replaced by a needs-based assessment that would probably benefit Wales but disadvantage Scotland. Other expert opinion agrees. The House of Lords Select Committee on the Barnett Formula, for example, recommended the adoption of a needs-based grants system allocated by 'a new independent expert body perhaps called the UK Funding Commission'. Whatever the outcome, Barnett would – at the very least – provide a convenient transitional model.

Borrowing powers for the Home Nations would also be a useful means by which the federation's component parts might deal with external shocks and fluctuations in revenue. Although such powers can cause problems (i.e. in the German Länder), with proper safeguards they can encourage fiscal prudence. The Scotland Act 2012 already equips the Scottish Government with the ability to borrow up to £2.2 billion to finance major capital projects, such as roads, hospitals and schools, while in early 2014 the UK Government announced those powers would be further boosted by giving the Holyrood administration direct access to capital funds with the ability to issue bonds.

A sensible safeguard would be a 'fiscal pact' agreed between the federal and Home Nation governments of a federal UK to define limits on borrowing and fiscal action, something the SNP accepts would be an inevitable feature of any 'currency union' between an independent Scotland and the rUK. Academic research even suggests federal states have significantly better performance than centralised states when it comes to central bank independence, quality of fiscal policies and institutions, prudent use of tax revenue, and public sector management, etc. But the wider point is well made by the Lib Dems, that tax cuts and extra borrowing need to be paid for – there is no 'free ride'. 'Home rule all round', they add, 'should mean responsible government all round.'

Income tax

As the former Labour and SNP MP Jim Sillars wrote in his recent book, *In Place of Fear II*, income tax is 'progressive and redistributive'. It is also the single largest source of Treasury revenue, constituting around 30 per cent of the total (followed by National Insurance contributions at around 20 per cent), which makes its absence from mainstream political debate – especially the emphasis on reducing inequality – all the more curious. Indeed, the debate is often back to front: those who bang on about reducing inequality often move seamlessly onto advocating tax cuts. As Jim Sillars puts it:

> There are those today who would place themselves well to the Left, who revel in their self-proclaimed radicalism, and love to rant against neo-liberalism, who are as intellectually sterile as those Labour failures. Rhetoric is not policy, and nor is policy when it avoids the realities.

Alas, Scottish politics is awash with rhetoric masquerading as policy and often avoids politically difficult economic realities. This phenomenon is compounded by a stifling orthodoxy that cuts across Left and Right, Nationalist and Unionist, that taxes must only ever go down or stay the same, never up. There is endless talk of gaining control of 'fiscal levers', although it appears the intention is only ever to move them downward. As the former Cabinet Secretary Gus O'Donnell reflected ruefully: 'Everyone wants to spend more and tax less, and at the national level that does not add up to a sustainable fiscal policy.'

Certain pro-independence voices, meanwhile, give the impression that an independent Scotland would somehow be able to escape all the wickedness of a modern globalised economy, a sort of Scottish exceptionalism. This is not, to say the least, very helpful. Furthermore, the biggest voice making that independence proposition – the SNP – argues that inequality can be tackled via orthodox neoliberal economic policy: a tweak here and a tweak there, and all will be well.

The trouble is, we have been here before: just as the New Right believed trickle-down economics would enrich everyone during the 1980s, the Blairite 'Third Way' advocated skimming off the proceeds from free market economics to redistribute wealth. Both worked in specific respects; for good or ill the former turned thousands of working-class citizens into property-owners and gave them hitherto unknown material wealth, while the latter – through tax and pension credits, etc – achieved genuine below-the-radar redistribution of wealth. But at the same time overall inequality increased from the late 1970s onwards and it is the stated aim of the SNP to reverse this trend.

But stating such an intent, the 'rhetoric' of Jim Sillars' aphorism, is not the same as having a 'policy' that will actually achieve that outcome. In truth, tackling inequality at this stage in the economic cycle would be enormously challenging even were the political will to exist (itself a questionable assumption). Sure, the Nordic economies offer alternative paths, but they are not without their own (increasing) demographic challenges and have a much older provenance based on a more substantial tax base derived from higher personal taxation, a point constantly and shamefully ducked by proponents of the Scandinavian model (even the ostentatiously left-wing Reid Foundation insists no tax rises would be necessary to implement its policy ideas). Lesley Riddoch's recent book, *Blossom*, virtually ignores economics.

Redistribution

It is time to get real. If those committed to reducing inequality are not seriously prepared to use existing and forthcoming tax-varying powers, reform property taxation or radically increase welfare payments, then the honest thing to do would be to say nothing at all, rather than promising the moon on a questionable fiscal basis.

A growing body of literature has convincingly argued that growing inequality in the UK, US and other developed nations is not only bad in itself, but bad for economic growth. Most famously, Richard Wilkinson and Kate Pickett made this claim in their 2009 book *The Spirit Level: Why Equality is Better for Everyone*, an argument more recently examined by Joseph Stiglitz (who serves on the Scottish Government's Council of Economic Advisers) in his 2012 polemic, *The Price of Inequality*. Although this theory has of course been challenged, it still provides a compelling backdrop to the current political debate – or rather lack of debate – in Scotland and the UK.

In a personal piece for the *Financial Times* in early 2014, Jonathan Ostry, deputy director of the International Monetary Fund's (IMF) research department, noted the general reluctance of policy makers to take serious steps to reverse inequality given their fear it would stunt economic growth. 'For most policy makers,' he wrote, 'redistribution has a bad name: a false cure that may be worse than the disease of inequality itself.' But when he and his colleagues, Andrew Berg and Haris Tsangarides, set out to test the theory that sharing wealth more equally might actually help produce more wealth overall, they reached two 'striking' conclusions.

Firstly, they found more unequal societies had slower and more fragile economic growth, growth being faster in more equal societies than in less equal ones, and regardless of whether they had highly redistributive tax systems. Secondly, the researchers found little evidence that a 'modestly redistributive' tax system had an adverse effect on growth. While highly redistributive systems might 'crimp' economic performance, moderate redistribution had 'negligible direct effects' on growth. Putting these two observations together, concluded Ostry *et al*, it led to the following important conclusion for policy:

> Making the tax system modestly more redistributive seems to have little direct effect on growth. Over time, however, it will result in a more equal distribution of income – and that, in turn, seems to lead to higher growth. Taking into account the direct effect of redistribution, and the indirect effect that operates through reduced inequality, we find that average levels of redistribution are associated with higher and more durable growth. Even large redistributions – undertaken presumably with the goal of improving equality – do not seem to carry a clear growth cost.

Interestingly, redistribution need not necessarily depend upon progressive taxation, but rather overall levels. They key point is that a higher overall tax take is required to fund transfers that reduce inequality. The SNP argues that economic growth fuelled by a competitive tax regime would, over time, increase the tax base and therefore the revenue available to an independent Scottish Government, which is – as outlined above – a decidedly orthodox economic view.

But when researchers at Stirling University, funded by the Economic and Social Research Council, looked at a series of tax and welfare levers which Scottish ministers might pull in order to reduce the gap between rich and poor, it concluded that many of the mechanisms required to do so – particularly property taxation – were already under the Scottish Parliament's control. And while independence would inevitably present policy makers with a 'more powerful set of levers', inequality could only be seriously tackled via 'substantial increases' to out-of-work benefits, a new universal basic income and a flat tax of 56 per cent applied to everything else.

'Radical changes' like these, the paper concluded with considerable understatement, would be 'politically difficult', but nevertheless the levers to reduce inequality already exist, to a degree, under the status quo and even more so under independence or a federal set-up; the real point is whether there is any public appetite or enough political will to see them being pulled. Dr David Comerford of Stirling University also acknowledged another problem, that given Scotland's 'high degree of integration with the rest of the UK... such policy change could trigger migration between countries'.

This would obviously be a problem, even under a federal UK, although arguably less so than at present given the greater fiscal autonomy implicit in a federation and the existence of equalising transfers. Even so, none of this is an argument – in itself – against higher taxes, a necessity if the goal is a higher overall tax take. It is difficult, particularly given the tax reductions enjoyed by higher earners over the last 35 years, to argue that no one in Scotland (and indeed across the whole of the UK) could afford to pay a little more income tax. Even a 1p increase in the basic rate (as proposed by the SNP during the 1999 Scottish Parliament election campaign) would raise an additional £350 million in annual revenue, a not inconsiderable sum, and something that could be used to target inequality alongside a more progressive system of property taxation (as proposed, then abandoned, by Scottish Labour at the 2007 Holyrood election).

As with corporate taxation, there is limited evidence individuals would flee, even to other parts of a federal UK, should taxes rise modestly. In a study of revenue-maximising rates, the IMF found that virtually all its members could raise top rates considerably higher and bring in significant extra sums: in particular it concluded the UK could raise its rates to an optimal 60 per cent or more before it would lose more than it gained in additional revenue. *The New Palgrave Dictionary of Economics*, reviewing all the research, reckoned the famous Laffer Curve (under which revenue is supposed to increase as taxes are reduced) – of which the current First Minister spoke approvingly a decade ago – does not kick in until about 75 per cent.

More to the point, as the Holtham Commission observed, the UK currently has 'a strikingly low proportion of tax revenue collected at the sub-national level, even by the standards of unitary states'. Three European Union member states, for example, levy sub-national taxes on corporate income, while six do so on personal income. Canada and the US, meanwhile, both allow both personal and corporate income taxes to vary sub-nationally. Holtham concluded:

> However, it appears possible for relatively small sub-national states or regions to operate somewhat different tax policies from their neighbouring regions within an integrated economy. That said, such tax differences are likely to induce migration flows between regions, as well as behavioural responses in those who remain. Although their magnitudes are uncertain, both the migration and the behavioural response arc disproportionately likely among the affluent, while out-migration is also more likely to be the response of the young and highly skilled to a relatively high sub-national tax burden.

But equally, and this is a point increasingly made by a curious alliance of Plaid Cymru and the Welsh Conservative Party, lowering rates might serve to attract those 'affluent' individuals and workers to economically poorer parts of the UK, for example Wales.

So a federal UK would offer Scotland even greater flexibility to pull fiscal levers – both up and down – while redesigning its fiscal architecture with greater simplicity and equality in mind (another of Alex Salmond's economic advisers, Sir James Mirlees, published a holistic proposal via the Institute of Fiscal Studies in November 2010), but even that would require a greater degree of radicalism and political will than currently exists. As Will Hutton has written, both the 20th century's economic dogmas – socialism and neoliberalism – have demonstrably failed, 'and the quest is on for better ways of making capitalism work both for itself – and for workers, consumers and citizens'. Federalism would arguably offer the ideal constitutional framework for doing so.

CHAPTER 6

Educational Federalism

Our education system should help children out of the circumstances in which they were born, not lock them into the circumstances in which they were born. We need them to fly as high as their luck, their ability and their sheer hard graft can actually take them. And it isn't going to happen magically. Sir John Major, November 2013

Around the cabinet table, a majority, including myself, were privately educated... On the bench of our supreme court, in the precincts of the bar, in our medical schools and university science faculties, at the helm of FTSE 100 companies and in the boardrooms of our banks, independent schools are – how can I best put this – handsomely represented. Michael Gove, Education Secretary

'IN A BRITISH FEDERATION', David Melding has written, 'one would expect the field of education... to rest at the national level.' Indeed, even under the constitutional status quo education is perhaps the most federalised of all domestic responsibilities, with different systems operating in England (a mix of independent, grammar, comprehensives, 'free' schools, academies, etc), Scotland (independent and state), Northern Ireland (grammars, including state) and Wales (mainly state, including of course Welsh and Gaelic medium education).

This is reflected by the existence of four different education ministers in the UK including, ironically, a Scot (Michael Gove) responsible for English education and the Bromley-born Mike Russell running Scotland's, distinct in most respects since the 1707 Treaty of Union. Since 1999, meanwhile, education policy in the four Home Nations has continued to diverge. Under a federal constitution, therefore, there would be little change in this area, at least in administrative terms, but at the same time it might be hoped that federalism, as well as expanding the political imagination, might lead to more creative policy thinking.

Educational policy is a domain ripe for fresh ideas. For too long the complacent mantra that 'Scottish education is the best in the world' has held sway, and while it is a comforting thought, it is no substitute for actual policy. As Gerry Hassan has written, too many Scots 'do not want to confront difficult facts about the Scots and education, and prefer to find succour in the repetition of myth and cliché'. He added (in *Caledonian Dreaming*):

> There is the constant evoking by Scottish Government ministers of 'free tuition fees', and celebration of Scottish universities (and their world ratings), along with education at all levels, without beginning to face up to how they fall short. These accounts don't address how education lets too many Scots down, the barriers of exclusion in higher and further education making too many places exclusively the preserve of the middle class, and the question of where innovation and change comes from in the system.

Similarly, in his short book *In Place of Fear II*, the Labour-turned-Nationalist politician Jim Sillars said it was time 'to end the foolish claims that we have a world-class education system'. '[It] is not perfect or near to world class,' he added, 'and it is time this was admitted and new ideas allowed to flow in.'

Even since the creation of a Scottish Parliament, however, ideas have not tended to flow. Rather, and the same is true of health policy, successive Scottish education ministers – Labour and SNP – have sought to formulate policy in reaction to that south of the border. Rather than producing innovative thinking, this has more often than not led to stagnation, and while the current Curriculum for Excellence (despite its unhelpful Orwellian branding) is well intentioned and most likely a step in the right direction, ministerial intervention is at best conservative.

Which is not to say that avoiding certain English educational developments is necessarily a bad thing, for it is still far from clear that Michael Gove's 'free schools' revolution – which very much operates within a Blairite groove – will achieve its stated aim, i.e. closing the gap between private and public sector. In this, the (English) Education Secretary is certainly sincere, but that is not enough; the proof, to exploit a cliché, will be in the pudding. Making state schools as good as their independent counterparts has been a quixotic goal of Conservative education ministers since the late 1980s, but there has been markedly little progress towards making it a reality.

Other Conservatives (though not Gove), and even some on the Left, openly toy with restoring English grammar schools to their former pre-

Crosland/Thatcher status as a means of reducing educational inequality, but this too is nostalgia masquerading as action. The Chief Inspector of Schools (in England) Sir Michael Wilshaw reacted bluntly when he said that grammar schools were 'stuffed full of middle-class kids' and that anyone who believed creating more of them was 'going to increase social mobility' needed to look at the percentage of grammar school pupils in receipt of free school meals (just three per cent). Sir Michael even dismissed Northern Ireland's extensive network of grammar schools, pointing out that the six counties of Ulster ranked below England in international comparisons, not least because 'grammar schools might do well with 10 per cent of the school population, but everyone else does really badly'. In Scotland, meanwhile, the Conservatives continue to toy with 'voucher' schemes that evoke the 1980s, failing to appreciate that such models would generally advantage those who already benefit from the status quo: predominantly middle-class, motivated parents (and this is not a bad thing) who naturally 'want the best' for their children.

The triumph of independent schools

In a 2012 speech to independent school head teachers in Brighton, Michael Gove said the dominance of privately-educated individuals in UK society was 'morally indefensible' and demonstrated a 'deep problem in our country'. And politicians, he (rightly) added, had failed to tackle the issue with 'anything like the radicalism required'. He continued:

> More than almost any developed nation, ours is a country in which your parentage dictates your progress. Those who are born poor are more likely to stay poor and those who inherit privilege are more likely to pass on privilege in England than in any comparable country. For those of us who believe in social justice, this stratification and segregation are morally indefensible.

Although this might have sounded surprising coming from a privately-educated Conservative Cabinet minister, Gove was not the first to highlight such concerns from within his party. The Tory MP George Walden (Latymer Upper School), who served as Mrs Thatcher's Minister for Higher Education between 1985 and 1987, recalled in his memoirs that to even think about public school dominance 'was to break a parliamentary taboo'. He added:

> For the Tories, I had learned by now, private schools were a touchstone of loyalty to a certain idea of Britain – their Britain – and insofar

as there was a problem it had been solved by the Assisted Places Scheme. Like myself, they knew perfectly well that this sop to the masses tended to be snaffled up by the middle classes, but so what? After all, the middle classes, in their majority, voted for us.

Walden was not opposed to independent schools, indeed he educated his own children in the private sector, but what he felt was 'wrong and deeply damaging was to behave like most liberal-minded columnists, who claimed they were against selection, then educated their children privately, or like many a Tory, who thought comprehensives were good enough for the others, but not for them'. He continued:

> I did not want to close private schools, but to open them up, on a voluntary basis, while maintaining their independence – something I knew by then from talking to private-school heads, especially in the ex-direct grant sector was not as crazy as it appeared. Such explanations dispelled some of my colleagues' incomprehension, but increased their fear. For many Tories there was only one thing worse than abolishing independent schools and that was to keep them – while making them accessible to all the talents. If that were to happen, how could they be sure that their own children would get in?

We shall return to Walden's aim of making private schools 'accessible to all the talents' in a moment, but first it is worth considering the situation in Scotland. The proportion of children educated privately north of the border is only 4.7 per cent of the total (compared with around 7 per cent in England), and at the beginning of the 2011–12 session there were more than 31,000 pupils attending independent schools.[1]

Although fewer children are educated privately in Scotland vis-à-vis England, there are quite striking regional variations, for example in Edinburgh almost a quarter of secondary school pupils are educated at fee-paying institutions; 'what school did you go to?' remains a very Edinburgh question (just look at the players' biographies at any Murrayfield fixture). Curiously, however, Scotland's independent schools – which after all educated the heir to the throne (Gordonstoun) and the last Prime Minister but one (Fettes) – do not feature as prominently in Scottish discourse as do

---

1 Scottish education is unusually homogenous within the independent and state school sectors; only Jordanhill in Glasgow stands out, funded by the Scottish Government but charging no fees despite being independent of its local authority.

Eton, Harrow *et al* south of the border. 'Under the comprehensive ethos,' observed Raymond Ross in the *Times Educational Supplement* a few years ago, 'fee-paying schools are the elephant in the room which everyone can see but few educationalists will address.' (Prior to the 1999 Scottish Parliament election, 29 per cent of Scots believed private education should be banned compared with 19 per cent in England, but thereafter fee-paying became less potent an issue.)

Indeed, the belief that Scotland was somehow 'different' in this respect holds sway even among centre-left columnists in London. The *Guardian*'s Jonathan Freedland, for example, observed in the *New York Review of Books* that 'Scotland has only a few private schools', when there are 'a few' in Aberdeen alone. Using the demographic composition of the Scottish Parliament vis-à-vis the House of Commons as a measurement, many in Scotland conclude that public school dominance simply is not as much of a problem as in England, but even at Holyrood MSPs are four times as likely to have attended a private school as those they represent (17 per cent, compared with 34 per cent at Westminster).

Indeed, two former Presiding Officers count among their ranks (George Watson's and Eton), as do two former Labour leaders (Glasgow Academy and George Watson's). As Professor Michael Keating concluded: 'The figures for the number of privately educated MSPs probably represents the elite of society as a whole. You would find the same thing in business or law. These numbers do demonstrate that MSPs are not socially representative.' And when 400 teenagers gathered in Dundee in August 2011 for the World Schools Debating Championships, members of the Scotland team were all privately educated.

But while at Westminster, where the dominance of public schools is generally acknowledged and discussed if not adequately tackled, in Scotland it is barely even mentioned. Education Secretary Mike Russell (Marr College, state) does not dwell on it while the Scottish Government's 2013 'White Paper' on independence – which prided itself on dealing with virtually every policy aspect of its constitutional vision – does not mention the independent sector once. At a private dinner with a senior SNP minister in late 2013 I was struck when, on being challenged about the issue by a (privately-educated) businessman, the minister in question said his questioner ought to regard the White Paper's silence as 'a bonus... a gain by omission'.

It is equally striking that discussion of private education in Scotland has arguably decreased as inequality – and especially consideration of inequality – has markedly *increased*. The only aspect which gets an airing of any sort is the charitable status of independent schools, which subsidises such institutions to the tune of £10 million a year, as opposed to state comprehensives (including those in Scotland's most deprived areas) which are charged full rates by local authorities from the public purse. Jim Sillars has argued that rather than withdrawing this status from private schools, as some propose, it ought to be extended to all state schools, which although under control of ministers, in Sillars' words, 'far outstrip the independent schools in terms of delivering a public benefit'.

Indeed, the Charities and Trustee Investment (Scotland) Act might sound unexciting, but it has actually become the means by which Scotland's independent schools might be compelled to open themselves up beyond their natural recruiting ground. Once passed in 2005 it set in motion a process under which the Office of the Scottish Charities Regulator (OSCR) investigated the 'public benefit' which legally justifies charitable status, and eventually 12 schools ended up having to meet criteria mainly to do with widening access, with funds previously reserved for scholarships awarded on the basis of an entrance test instead being channelled into means-tested bursaries.

Now as the Scottish Council for Independent Schools (SCIS) points out, there are significant savings to the public purse of educating around 31,000 children in the independent sector (it claims to 'save' the state more than 35 times as much as it receives in financial benefits), and this is undeniably true, but it does not adequately address the inequality point, which is undeniably strong. In an important essay for the *New Statesman* in early 2014 (illustrated with a large photograph of Edinburgh's Fettes), the historian David Kynaston and his son George focused on the British Left and its obvious discomfort with the issue, but also attempted to define what, in essence, was the problem. 'They matter', concluded the Kynastons of independent schools (one of whom was state educated, the other not), 'because of their continued dominance, acting as a roadblock both to upward and (less often noted) downward social mobility.' They added:

> All this is not just down to talent and 'character'. There is a systematic process at work of giving better educational – and subsequently professional – opportunities to those already from the best-off backgrounds. Although private schools educate only 7 per cent of the population, their students take up almost half the places at Oxbridge and one-third of the places across the whole Russell Group [which represents 24 of the UK's 'leading' universities]. According to the education charity the Sutton Trust, an independent day school student is 55 times more likely to win a place at Oxbridge and 22 times more likely to go to a top-ranked university than a state school

student from a poor household. It is not just education that the parental chequebook buys but the assumption of a substantial socio-economic premium. There are, after all, only so many available rungs on the ladder.

The essay went on to skilfully dismantle most of the standard arguments for retaining the status quo, that independent schools, through grants and bursaries, were actually tackling inequality ('the overwhelming majority of students at private schools are still fee-paying, and most of these students are paying the full amount'); that parents make 'sacrifices' to put their children through private school ('If you are in a position to pay fees, or even a substantial portion of fees, you are far removed from the reality of most parents'); the real problem lies with the state sector ('80 per cent of which is now rated good or outstanding'); and, of course, the libertarian argument of parents' 'right to choose' ('a phantom right for most people, given that fees are not an option'). After all, wrote the Kynastons,

> It is not the child's money that is spent on fees; no child has earned the right to a better education, just as no child has failed to earn that right. It is a question of liberty – the maximum possible liberty consistent with a like liberty for others. Do some parents have the right to pay for an education that indirectly harms the life chances of other children by blocking their path?

And that really is the fundamental point: independent schools, be they in Scotland or the rest of the UK, do not exist in isolation, benefiting (or not) only those who attend them; they indirectly damage the prospects of the 93 per cent of children – in other words the overwhelming majority – who are educated in the state sector, not just when it comes to university admissions (as explored below), but thereafter in terms of access to professional occupations, lifetime earnings and in a myriad of other related ways. Any examination of the issue, therefore, has to tackle that reality, not skirt around it.

No one is talking about abolition. In a democratic society it is neither possible nor desirable to prevent parents paying for their child's education if that is what they want to do. 'The question is not whether these schools should exist,' write the Kynastons. 'We are where we are. The question is, are they educating the wrong children? And how do we end the divide to make them part of the common weal?' Indeed, most independent schools are demonstrably excellent institutions. As Alasdair Roberts observed in the 2013 edition of the book *Scottish Education*, although the 'exam success of independent schools may be partly explained by the social class of parents', beyond any 'parent effect' the 'positive outcomes due to private education's dedication to achievement can scarcely be doubted'. Only an educational vandal would seriously want to abolish that dedication and track record of achievement; it is self-evidently valuable, yet equally self-evidently it presently benefits too narrow a section of the Scottish and UK population. It is very easy to defend the excellence of public schools; much less easy to defend who benefits from that excellence.

But there is little or no evidence that widening access to independent schools – which must surely be the aim – would seriously compromise quality (even accepting that that, in itself, is a reasonable counter-argument). Widening access is of course a vague aim but one that appears to attracting a growing consensus. Although there has been both gentle persuasion (in September 2011 David Cameron urged head teachers from leading private schools to do more to justify their charitable status and reduce educational apartheid) and subtle coercion (such as that practised by OSCR north of the border), it does not go nearly far enough. In an ideal world, one might argue, private sector intake would mirror that of society as a whole, but given that politics is the art of the possible rather than the theoretically possible, one must settle upon a proportion.

This is inevitably arbitrary, but several commentators and educational experts have spoken of a quarter, or 25 per cent, which seems a good place to start. To an extent, this revisits the old Assisted Places Scheme (APS), basically state-funded places at private schools, which existed from 1980 until abolished (curiously) by the first government of Tony Blair. The prominent *Times* columnist (and former Conservative MP) Matthew Parris has promoted this idea, as has Peter Lampl of the Sutton Trust (which churns out cogent analysis of educational inequality in the UK) and more surprisingly Anthony Seldon of Wellington College, a rare proponent of change from within the private sector. Seldon's report for the Social Market Foundation *Schools United*, argued that such a move 'enhances social mobility, ends the divide between state and independent schools, engages parents far more fully... and ensures all young people have much richer opportunities, regardless of family background'.

There were, of course, obvious problems with the APS, for – much like grammar schools – its impact upon social mobility was illusory, generally benefiting children of motivated middle-class parents with relatively modest means. It also benefited a tiny proportion of state pupils and, as Labour rightly argued in 1997, public money ought to 'benefit the many, not just the few'.

Citing this as a precedent, Matthew Parris argued:

We must punch a great big gaping hole through the walls surrounding the independent sector and let non-fee-paying children in. Unlike the Sutton Trust I don't think this should be voluntary or gradualist, or weaker independent schools will accept the lion's share. All private schools, both boarding and day schools, all of which are charities, should be forced by law to accept 25 per cent of their intake as scholarship boys and girls, funded by the State on a means-tested basis. Unless we reverse silly prohibitions of academic selection, this would have to be done by ballot. Independent schools' selection processes are pretty opaque anyway.

Under Lampl's proposal for 'open access', meanwhile, roughly a third of places at independent day schools would be fully funded and another third partly funded; something he believes more than 80 such schools would be willing to sign up to. Now Messrs Parris, Seldon and Lampl are unlikely revolutionaries, and while their respective proposals might appear radical, it is difficult to think what form the contrary argument would take (after all, access would remain quite significantly unequal). And to those who argue that such a move would be impractical, just look at India: in 2012 its elite private schools, many established in the 19th century and modelled on the British public school system, were instructed to reserve a quarter of their places for poorer pupils. Several of the schools mounted a legal challenge to the government's legislation, but their objections were over-ruled by the Indian Supreme Court.

That would obviously be a last resort, while government (be it federal or Home Nation) could also be proactive in other areas. Another approach, as outlined in Andrew Adonis's 2012 book *Education, Education, Education*, is to draw private day schools into the state sector as direct-grant academies, thus retaining their 'ethos' and autonomous governance but dropping fees and academic selection, a route already taken by six schools including the prestigious Liverpool College, a moment Adonis describes as 'perhaps the single biggest breach in the Berlin Wall between the private and state sectors of education in recent decades'. Given sufficient political backing, Adonis believes as many as 100 other schools might follow Liverpool's lead.

Another aspect of the Adonis proposals is making every private school the 'sponsor' of an academy, the idea being to leverage the expertise, influence and resources of the private sector into improving state schools and in the process lessening the divide between the two sectors. Eton and Wellington are prominent in this movement, although as Adonis himself concedes progress beyond that is 'agonisingly' slow; Michael Wilshaw told private school heads at the Headmasters' and Headmistresses' Conference (HMC) that their existing partnerships with state schools largely amounted to 'crumbs off your tables, leading more to famine than feast', and he had a point. He also told them that 'if you believe, as so many of your original founders believed, that how you deal with wider society and how you relate to those children less fortunate than your students defines you as schools', then much more had to be done.

And far from being a solution for a specifically 'English' problem, all of the above is just as pertinent in Scotland, even in the absence of academies and grammars, particularly in its educationally stratified capital. As a 2012 investigation by the *Guardian* newspaper revealed, Edinburgh has one of the worst records for getting poorer children into Scotland's top universities, with only 1.4 per cent of children from its poorest neighbourhoods (and attending a state school) achieving three or more As in Highers, the minimum needed for many top universities or degree courses. As Lindsay Paterson, professor of educational policy at Edinburgh University, observed, it was not 'just that Edinburgh's figures are extremely low but that the inequality in Edinburgh is extremely high'.

In most of Scotland's urban areas segregated social housing and the 'vagaries' of catchment areas (particularly in Edinburgh, where the boundaries for Boroughmuir and Gillespie's defy geographical credibility) create highly socially stratified schools that compound inequalities in society. Jim Sillars has also written of 'schools in areas where there is virtually no social mix, where social stress and deprivation is the norm, where children are born to fail and where upward social mobility is not even a dream'. Education should offer a means of reducing these uncomfortable realities, not making them worse. An important first step in a Scottish context would be acknowledging they exist at all.

As the Kynastons concluded in their *New Statesman* essay (and remember they were writing from a left-of-centre perspective): 'There is a moment to be seized.'

> The loosening up of the state system through academies and free schools has blown away the old plea of the private schools to be left alone in splendid, independent isolation; social mobility is going backwards; the question of our rich/poor divide in education has been spotlighted not only by the make-up and social background of our current cabinet but also by the increased profile of organisations such as Teach First, dedicated to enhancing equality of opportunity. While on the left we have the haunting, ever more distant memory of

1945, with the knowledge that missed opportunities take a very long time to come round again.

The myth of tuition fees

Complacency, alas, extends beyond secondary-level education, and indeed the relative dominance of public schools naturally filters through to higher (much more than further) education. Again, the figures speak for themselves. Forty per cent of all entrants to St Andrews University are privately educated – not far off the 50 per cent recorded at Oxbridge – 30 per cent at Edinburgh and even at Aberdeen, my *alma mater*, it is 20 per cent. And again, this is not generally discussed, for Oxbridge dominates the relevant discourse, fuelling the general impression that educational inequality is more of a problem south of the border; the myth (and it is clearly a myth) that most children in Scotland attend a good local comprehensive and then progress to university retains a strong and arguably damaging grip on the Scottish psyche. (Intriguingly, graduates of Glasgow University dominate Holyrood to a greater extent than Oxbridge does the House of Commons, accounting for a quarter of all MSPs.)

Since 1999 Scottish politicians (of most political hues) have hidden behind the mantra 'no tuition fees' as a panacea for all higher educational ills, but underneath the rhetoric not only are the differences between the Scottish and English systems not as stark as often presumed, but in terms of increasing access, the gradual abolition of tuition fees over the past decade and a half has actually had a minimal impact. Not only did figures released by the Scottish Government in 2012 show that only 220 of the poorest children from across Scotland, defined as being from the bottom fifth of deprived areas by postcode, achieved grades good enough to apply for university places (a mere 50 were able to apply to Oxbridge), but very few managed to win a place at Scotland's 'ancient' universities (Edinburgh, Glasgow, Aberdeen and St Andrews); particular opprobrium attached itself to St Andrews in Fife, where just 13 children from such backgrounds gained admittance.

Now of course Scottish universities should not be compelled to admit students without adequate grades, although several studies comparing state-educated university students to their privately schooled counterparts with similar exam results have shown the former outperform the latter, so there is a strong argument for gauging potential rather than exam prowess when it comes to handling the transition from school to university. To be fair, (Scottish) Education Secretary Mike Russell has told the ancients to do more to increase admission rates for poorer students (even threatening fines if they fail to do so), but that does not address wider issues concerning the dogma of free tuition.

Clearly, when most students attending university are from middle-class backgrounds then middle-class families will benefit most from not having to pay fees that, it must be assumed, many could otherwise afford. It is often forgotten that the original Blair-era tuition fees regime (which applied for a few years in Scotland as well as in the rest of the UK) was means tested, a fact which in itself guaranteed opposition, but at the same time it meant roughly a third of students paid nothing, another third paid something and the remaining third paid the full whack, then a relatively modest £1,000 a year. The initial Scottish Executive (as it then was) policy actually compelled *all* students to pay a 'graduate endowment' – with a painfully low earnings threshold – which was arguably more punitive than the system it replaced, although that subtlety was lost in the euphoria of the first devolved government having 'scrapped' tuition fees.

But I digress. Once one conquers understandable aversion to means testing (which, after all, is a reality in several other areas), the argument against predominantly middle-class (and therefore higher earning, both potentially and in parental terms) students paying fees becomes rather difficult to sustain. As the blogger Graeme Cowie examined in a 2012 blog, while Scottish students accumulated an average debt of £18,000 and English students between £37,500 and £43,000, given that Scots had to start repaying theirs at a lower income threshold – £15,795 versus £21,000 in England – this produced a Scottish system that was actually *more* regressive, particularly for those on lower incomes. This presumably was not the intention of successive Scottish lawmakers.

So what can be done to broaden access and reduce inequality if free tuition does not appear to be the game-changer many assumed it would be? As Michael Wilshaw told the Headmasters' and Headmistresses' Conference (in what could have been interpreted as a friendly warning), the alternative to broadening access to private schools would be to concentrate their minds through university quotas that actively reduced their socio-economic premium. University College London has already gone down this route, while the University of Edinburgh generated predictable controversy by announcing that it was to begin considering the family background of applicants (many of those objecting presumably had similar qualms about the admissions process for Edinburgh's independent schools).

Again, in an ideal world Scotland's (and indeed the UK's) top universities would award places in a ratio closer to that of the population as a whole. But, again, one must operate within realistic boundaries, and Richard Wilkinson and Kate Pickett (of *Spirit Level* fame) have suggested compelling universities to randomly allocate places to the highest-ranked applicants from each school. They explain:

> So pupils in the top 10 or 20 per cent coming from schools in the poorest areas would have the same chances as pupils in the top 10 or 20 per cent from Eton. Evidence shows that students from state schools do better at university than privately educated students with the same A-level grades, so this may raise rather than lower educational standards. This could be introduced to cover a low percentage from each school and then raised gradually. Each university would allocate places randomly among pupils who were among the best from each school applying to that university. There are several international examples of successful schemes similar to this.

Indeed, unlikely inspiration comes from Texas, which guarantees a place at (a state) university to the top ten per cent of pupils at every state school, an unusually progressive policy for a traditionally – and staunchly – Republican part of America. In the United States this, and other interventionist policies usually geared towards African-Americans, is known as 'affirmative action', not a bad description of what is arguably required in Scotland and the UK, but not just for ethnic minorities but an even larger section of society – the underprivileged.

Equality in public life

In a much-publicised speech towards the end of 2013 the former Conservative Prime Minister Sir John Major told Tory activists that he found the dominance of a private-school educated elite in the UK 'truly shocking'. 'In every single sphere of British influence,' he added for good measure, 'the upper echelons of power in 2013 are held overwhelmingly by the privately educated or the affluent middle class. To me from my background, I find that truly shocking.'

Although there were obvious criticisms of Sir John's intervention – chiefly his own record as Prime Minister and his partisan attempt to pin the problem on the Labour Party – he of course spoke nothing less than the truth. Again the statistics are well worn. With only 7 per cent of the UK's children educated privately they go on to provide 37 per cent of Olympic athletes, 35 per cent of MPs, 54 per cent of journalists and around 70 per cent of High Court judges. As Michael Gove put it with considerable understatement, they are 'handsomely represented' in public life, not to mention in the worlds of sport, music, comedy, television and theatre. And in Scotland, as elsewhere in the UK, these groups disproportionately fill up middle-class professions such as accountancy, medicine and law; recent research by the Law Society of Scotland, for example, found that nearly a third of its members had attended an independent school (although it noted the proportion appeared to be falling over time).

But as Gove was careful to point out in the course of his remarks, none of what he highlighted was intended to 'decry the individuals concerned or criticise the schools they attended'. Undeniably, he added, such professionals were 'hugely talented and the schools they attended are premier league institutions, but the sheer scale, the breadth and the depth of private school dominance of our society points to a deep problem in our country'. So what of the solution? Gove's is to create 'free schools' which will, over time, compete with those in the private sector and thus level the playing field, but this is both questionable (quality is an issue) and as yet unquantifiable, although a combination of the proposals outlined above – at school and university level – ought, if successful, to reverse ever-decreasing social mobility.

Even so, further action at the point at which graduates enter the labour market is probably desirable, although much trickier to design and implement. Richard Wilkinson and Kate Pickett have suggested ensuring that job selection procedures and professional associations should be 'charged with the duty of monitoring progress and taking action against offending institutions', while Alan Milburn, in his guise as the Coalition's social mobility tsar, has recommended that internships (predominantly the preserve of the 'affluent middle class') might be made subject to same rules as the wider labour market or, going further, made part of a national internship service, so work experience was not just divided much more equitably, but also seen to be so.

Such ideas are, usefully, no longer the preserve of the Left, with David Skelton arguing that 'Conservatism is at its best when it's focused on spreading opportunity, and at its worst when it's seen as defensively defending vested interests and privilege'. The right-leaning think tank Policy Exchange even argued that equality law should include 'class' to ensure that middle-class professionals did not dominate UK public life. Dr Michael Pinto-Duschinsky, lead author of the report, said: 'It is vital for a functioning democracy that all its citizens are represented in public life. It's shameful that working-class communities are being excluded from sitting on public bodies.'

This chapter has strayed far from the somewhat narrower constitutional subject of this short book. A federalised UK with Scotland as one of its

Home Nations would not, of course, guarantee that education would be adequately reformed to produce a more equal society, for constitutional change can only ever be a means to an end rather than an end in itself (something many Nationalists fail to appreciate). But perhaps, as John Barnes argued in his 1998 pamphlet, UK federalism will allow 'new and sometimes unfashionable ideas to flourish'. For the reasons outlined above, in the field of education policy it is badly needed.

CHAPTER 7

Welfare Federalism

WHEN A FEDERAL solution to the governance of the United Kingdom was first discussed seriously about a century ago the Welfare State as we understand it today existed only in nascent form. It had begun to emerge during the 1906–14 Liberal governments, which included the passing of the Old-Age Pensions Act in 1908 and the enacting of the National Insurance Act in 1911, which set up a National Insurance contribution for unemployment and health benefits.

Although the latter was ostentatiously 'National' it was actually, at least initially, administered on a Home Nation basis, with Scottish, Welsh and Irish Commissioners controlling the insurance scheme from 'central' offices in Edinburgh, Cardiff and Dublin. As the legislation made clear:

> All sums received from contributions under this Part of this Act in respect of insured persons resident in Scotland, and all sums paid out of moneys provided by Parliament in respect of benefits under this Part of this Act to such persons, and the expenses of administration of such benefits shall be paid into a fund to be called the Scottish National Health Insurance Fund, under the control and management of the Scottish Insurance Commissioners.

The 1911 Act also made provision for a 'joint committee' of National Insurance Commissioners, whose powers were to include

> making regulations as to the valuation of societies and branches which have amongst their members persons resident in England, Scotland, Ireland, and Wales, or any two or any three of such parts of the United Kingdom, and the regulations so made shall require that,

for the purposes of the provisions of this Part of this Act relating to valuations, surpluses, deficiencies and transfers, the members resident in each such part shall be treated as if they formed a separate society.

This decentralised, federalised system of welfare lasted for more than 30 years until it was centralised by Clement Attlee's post-war government. Other early aspects of the Welfare State were also territorially specific, for example the Highlands and Islands Medical Service – established in 1913 – was a nascent National Health Service applying in one geographically remote part of the Scotland for almost 35 years. Although treatment was not free, fees were set at minimal levels and patients were still seen to even if they were unable to pay.

The point is that a 'national' (as in UK-wide) system of welfare need not necessarily be centrally controlled, and indeed was not for several decades during the previous century. Generally, however, the pattern of the Welfare State's development has led to more centralised control, even if that has not been mirrored by other constitutional developments. It is often forgotten that even the birth of the National Health Service (NHS) in 1948 had distinctive, and again quasi-federal, features. For example a separate Act covered Scotland, while in Northern Ireland – at that point administered by the maximally devolved Stormont parliament – universal health care was also applied in a distinctive fashion. Indeed, because the Government of Ireland Act, 1920, which governed devolution in the province, predated the Attlee reforms, welfare was applied separately in the six counties albeit in a fashion closely mirroring that on the mainland. To this day, however, the Northern Ireland Assembly retains the power to alter certain aspects of social security payments, a historical overhang from its Stormont-era autonomy.

Since the devolutionary reforms of 1998/99, meanwhile, further elements of the Welfare State have been decentralised. The Scottish NHS, long under the administrative jurisdiction of the old Scottish Office, came under the Scottish Parliament's remit, while the NHS in Northern Ireland fell under Assembly control and to a more limited degree that of the NHS in Wales under the guidance of the National Assembly in Cardiff. As the 2009 Calman Commission observed,

the welfare state is not all provided, like social security, on a uniform national basis of cash entitlements to individuals according to their circumstances. In general, where welfare is provided in the form of services, these were decentralised and are now devolved.

The devolution of healthcare was in itself significant, but it was not accompanied by the decentralisation of welfare more generally, the prevailing political consensus holding that that was best reserved as a UK-wide or federal level function.

Well, at least most of it. The 2012 Welfare Reform Act, for example, indirectly provided the Scottish Parliament with additional welfare responsibilities, including the transfer of revenue associated with the old social fund, community care grants and crisis loans (scrapped throughout the UK as of 1 April 2013) to the Scottish Government. Ministers at Holyrood opted to channel these into a new 'Scottish Welfare Fund', while responsibility for council tax reduction (which replaced the old council tax benefit scheme), was another power that passed to Holyrood more or less unnoticed. Together with control of prescriptions (which are now free of charge, as in Wales), the NHS and personal care for the elderly, it could be said that by 2014 Scotland already found itself in control of considerable *Scottish* welfare state.

The constitutional lawyer Professor Adam Tomkins also observed the tension between powers already devolved and reserved elements of welfare:

> If there are parts of the social security budget that are closely tied to substantive powers already devolved to Holyrood, then there is at least a powerful prima facie reason for considering their transfer to Edinburgh. Public housing is a devolved responsibility in Scotland, for example. So why not devolve housing benefit? Likewise, social care is a matter for which Scottish Ministers are responsible in Scotland. So why not devolve the attendance allowance? And so on.

Welfare Unionism

Others are more cautious. In 2013 the academic and former civil servant Jim Gallagher delivered a lecture called 'Hanging Together' at Glasgow University that set out the case for what he elsewhere termed 'welfare unionism', the orthodox belief that most welfare functions are best delivered at the UK/federal level. As he put it:

> Because we have an integrated fiscal system we are used to the idea that public expenditure should go wherever the need is in the country. Poor areas shouldn't have rotten public services simply because than they do not have a strong local tax base. Pensioners should get the same support whether they live in the rich South East

the poor North West. Taxation should be redirected to support pensions, benefits and public services where needed, not one of the money arises.

Identifying both 'an instrumental' and 'a principled' argument, Gallagher posited that fiscal sharing created a 'sense of common obligation', enabling economic integration to connect with 'social solidarity'. He added:

> Need, not geography, has been the watchword of UK public spending for over 100 years. Ever since the poor laws were abolished, it's been British fiscal policy that local spending is not determined by local taxable capacity, like poor law ratepayers. Pensions, health and welfare services are supported by general taxation, levied across the country according to ability to pay.

Benefits, continued Gallagher, were a case in point, spending in different parts of the UK on pensions and unemployment payments being 'determined solely by individual entitlements'. 'To each according to his needs might have been a Marxist slogan,' he said, 'but spending according to need is now a principle widely accepted across the political spectrum.'

Gallagher also dwelled upon National Insurance, although seemingly unaware of its early administrative backstory:

> A social union pools not just resources but risks as well. This is a form of insurance. In insurance, the wider the risk pool, the more secure the benefits. UK National Insurance is the biggest insurance scheme of all. Being in a bigger insurance scheme matters. Take old-age pensions. The good news that we are all likely to live longer creates pressures on the payment of pensions. Scotland is getting older quicker than the rest of the UK. So the pressure here will be even greater. In UK national insurance, as resources are pooled, risks like this are shared too. Split the pool, you increase the risks – especially in the smaller part of it...

Gallagher's point was that a reformed Union had to 'retain the combination of economic integration and social solidarity that creates both the domestic market and a well functioning social market'. In his view that meant retaining a 'national system of national insurance'. The 'clue', he added, was 'in the name'.

The Welsh Conservative federalist David Melding shares Gallagher's caution about eroding too fully the reserved or federal responsibilities of a future UK. Any claim, he wrote in his e-book *The Reformed Union*, that the Scottish Parliament (and indeed the National Assembly) ought to control most welfare policy, if granted, 'would start to turn Britain into a loose confederation, not a federal state'. Likewise, the 2006 Steel Commission also concluded that the 'ability of the United Kingdom Government to make common provision across the UK for pensions and social security benefits acts as an automatic support for those in greatest need, bringing the resources of the union to bear in a way which supports areas of greatest economic and social need'.

Similarly, the more recent Scottish Liberal Democrat commission on federalism recommended that pensions and benefits remain a responsibility of the UK or federal government, although it perceived this as part of the 'partnership work' between the federal tier and Home Nations, noting that the new Universal Credit contained a number of existing benefits that straddled present Westminster and Holyrood responsibilities. Like Gallagher, it concluded that powers over the National Insurance system 'should be allocated to the UK, and subsequently federal level of government'. And while the 2009 Calman Commission recognised that it was 'in principle possible to envisage a Union in which such rights and responsibilities' were 'decentralised, and differ in different parts of the country', it also observed that even in federal states it was common (if not universally so) that welfare was a federal – rather than a state or provincial – responsibility.

Partnership working

The Liberal Democrats fleshed out their concept of 'partnership working' (echoed in Scottish Labour's 2014 devolution proposals) by explaining that the Scottish Government, and presumably the other Home Nations, might act as 'agents' for the federal government on specific projects: 'For example, it might make sense for a particular Department for Work and Pensions [DWP] programme on welfare to be run by the Scottish Government, utilising its local agencies and services to make it more effective.'

Given the existing concentration of DWP functions and offices in Scotland this would make a lot of sense under a federal set-up, not least when it comes to the UK Government's Work Programme; i.e. the cash payments to those seeking work would continue to be made by the UK government but with full responsibility for skills and training passing to the Home Nations. As the Scottish Liberal Democrats concluded, 'no single tier of government acting alone would be able to conquer' various social 'ills'.

The Labour-aligned Institute for Public Policy Research (IPPR), meanwhile, envisages the Scottish Parliament being granted sweeping powers over billions of pounds worth of welfare, including the right to control housing benefit, the Work Programme and attendance allowance, while the UK would retain control of pensions and Job Seekers' Allowance. As the IPPR's Guy Lodge put it, 'welfare devolution would improve policy without undermining the fundamental level of shared UK-wide social citizenship'. So while the current Welfare State already possesses a degree of flexibility and territorial diversity, a federal UK would inevitably expand the scope for further variation while retaining – as in other federal states around the world – basic minimum standards.

Tackling inequality and policy proposals

That the UK is the 'fourth most unequal country in the world' has recently become a mantra of Scottish political discourse and although it contains an element of truth, it is at the same time simplistic and, more to the point, unaccompanied by any serious plan of action. The UK's ranking in this respect depends upon the measurement used, i.e. income, income post-taxes and benefits, etc, while the growth on inequality over the past 35 years – although undeniable – is far from linear. Certain reforms introduced by the Labour governments of 1997–2010, for example the minimum wage, tax and pension credits, made a significant difference (something many on the Left are reluctant to acknowledge). But the general trend, of course, is worsening.

As noted in Chapter 5, any serious attempt to reduce inequality would generally have to involve more generous welfare. Political will in this respect, even in the SNP, appears to be lacking (even Alex Salmond has spoken approvingly of a 'cap'), but welfare federalism could at least clarify the social levers available to each level of government and offer scope for more creative policy thinking in this area. For example the second report of the Devo Plus commission, *Improving Social Outcomes in Scotland*, convincingly argued that responsibility for the delivery of what it called 'Social Welfare' ought to be made clear at each level of government.

And while it did not advance any specific welfare policy, it did argue that Scotland (since 1999) had 'failed to match relative economic improvement with increased social justice and better social outcomes', not least because the 'split in programmes' between Westminster and Holyrood meant that policy in relation to alleviating poverty had been 'unfocussed and inefficient'. Therefore it saw merit in allowing Scotland (and presumably, in due course, the other Home Nations) greater control over 'discretionary benefits' or 'additional payments', provided this was financed 'out of own resource' and 'done in a way that is in addition to (and not detract from) the UK entitlements'. As it explained:

> The reform agenda, and the constitutional debate allows us to look to create a clearer explanation to beneficiaries of support where the benefits come from and what entitlement exists. This 'social charter' should be put in place and allows for a connection to be made in people's minds that they are receiving UK support regardless of where they live, but if the politicians they elect choose to supplement this, there is clarity as to how it is funded. Crucially, it also reflects the appropriate level of government providing the appropriate level of support.

Specifically, Devo Plus recommended devolution of non-Universal Credit work programmes, attendance allowance, winter fuel payments, Job Centre Plus, social provision and carer's allowance to the Scottish Parliament, with funding provided via the Scottish block grant as part of any future equalisation mechanism.

Pensions

As already established, pensions would most likely remain a UK or federal responsibility, but that does not rule out significant reform. Indeed, the ticking time bomb of pension provision in Scotland and other parts of the UK is well established, although again proposals for sorting it out are less well defined.

The think tank Reform Scotland, however, proved itself rather more ambitious, proposing in February 2014 an 'entirely new pension system and structure'. This it called the Universal Contributory Pension (UCP), based on all workers paying a minimum of 8 per cent of their salary into a fully transferable pension pot chosen and owned by the worker. Such a system would also give discretion over retirement age to the worker, with the UK (or federal) government providing a flat rate of income tax relief and the pensions credit continuing to provide a minimum guarantee.

I say ambitious because Reform Scotland also argued that under the UCP policy National Insurance would be scrapped and income tax increased (initially) by 7p to cover the resulting decrease in revenue. And with the UCP applying to all workers in the public and private sectors, the existing state pension could be phased out over a period of 45 years. As Ben Thomson, chairman of Reform Scotland, explained, the problem with the present system was that those 'faithfully paying' into National Insurance and public sector occupational schemes had 'no ownership over their pension assets'. 'They are not paying into a personal pot for themselves,' added Thomson, 'they are paying for today's pensioners and are dependent on an increasingly stretched next generation to pay for them.'

The point, as in the case of local government reform and fiscal policy, is that a federal UK would offer the most flexible constitutional framework in which to innovate in terms of welfare provision. But some Unionists, even federalists, err on the side of caution when it comes to further decentralisation of the Welfare State, but they are being needlessly conservative, for not only have certain functions already been devolved to Scotland and Northern Ireland, but that looks likely to continue in the period following the independence referendum, whatever the result (the Scottish Government envisages a 'transitional' arrangement in this area). But the point is this: a federal UK could set the floor, but not necessarily the ceiling, entitling Scots to at least the same welfare benefits as those in the rest of the federation but, if the (Scottish) Home Nation legislated for and, of course, provided funding, then they may have access to additional entitlements as well.

CHAPTER 8

Conclusion

One thing which inspired me to take a fresh look at how Scotland could work is studying America. The United States system of government is far from perfect but it is dynamic, diverse and, above all, democratic... There will always be debates about where the precise line should be between states' rights and federal authority but... they're [all] proud to be Americans. As are Californians, New Yorkers and Texans.

Ruth Davidson, Scottish Conservative leader

[T]he United Kingdom will need to work out a more openly federal system. The Westminster Parliament could remain as an arena for determining a major cross-border issues... but a great deal of power, decision making and taxation would have to be devolved to the four national parliaments and to local and regional authorities.

Linda Colley, *Acts of Union and Disunion*

The present quasi-federalist settlement with Scotland is unsustainable...Why not devolve all responsibilities except foreign policy, defence and management of the economy.

Sir John Major, former Conservative Prime Minister

A new constitutional settlement is needed that embraces all parts of the country fairly and equally, possibly on a federal basis. It is at this point, not after the Scottish referendum, that debate about a positive alternative to separation should begin.

Lord Lexden (Conservative peer), *The Times*

The best way of shifting Britain towards greater economic rationality would be to retain the union and pound but to restructure the country into a federation. Each nation – Scotland, England, Wales and Northern Ireland – would be given its own parliament, extreme devolution and the power and responsibility to raise and spend all (or almost all) the money themselves.

Allister Heath, *City AM*

[We want] a vibrant Scotland within a federal independent Britain.

Nigel Farage, UKIP leader

Communists... continue to call for radical federalism as the best way of developing class cohesion across the nations of Britain: national parliaments with powers of economic intervention, ownership and control and a federal parliament with overall powers over economic policy and a constitutional obligation to redistribute in terms of social need.   Scottish Committee, Communist Party of Great Britain

Labour needs to articulate an alternative to independence... which is modern, looser, flexible, federal and recognises the wish of Scots for the best of all worlds, stopping well short of independence.   Henry McLeish, former First Minister of Scotland

[I]t is in the clear interests of the English voter, and the Tories, that the first steps are taken towards a federal UK. Within that new kingdom we can come together on issues of joint endeavour but be free to decide more policies at the level of England, Scotland, Wales and Northern Ireland.   Tim Montgomerie, the *Guardian*

The UK must continue down the road to becoming a federal nation.
                                        Carwyn Jones, First Minister of Wales

Salmond is offering a new British confederation in everything but name. There would be a free trade, a common currency, a common head of state, and a common security strategy through Nato... The common monetary system would anchor the confederation economically.   George Kerevan, former SNP candidate

I'm an out and out UK federalist... There was never a project for Welsh independence, anyway.   Lord Elis-Thomas, peer and former Plaid Cymru MP

If I were a Scot, I would be sorely tempted by the prospect of proper independence... There is, though, an attractive alternative: to use the SNP as a battering ram to create a more federal Britain with Scotland as the principal beneficiary.
                                        Will Hutton, the *Guardian*

An alternative, of course, would be a loose federation, with the English regions granted substantial autonomy, too, breaking the hegemony of Westminster across the islands... An old dream, yes. But still one worth fighting for.
                                        Owen Jones, *The Independent*

All the components are there, but their implications need to be better understood... it should be home rule all round and, as in federal countries worldwide, national parliaments should be funded by a mixture of a share of UK taxes, which give effect to social solidarity, and their own tax resources.   Jim Gallagher, Better Together

[Michael] Moore and his Liberal Democrat party stand for a federal UK, and federalism would give people in Scotland a great deal of what we want. However, a federal UK is, in reality, out of reach.   Stephen Noon, Yes Scotland

OPENING THE CONCLUSION to this short book with so many quotes might look heavy handed but the point is an important one: to counter the suggestion that somehow federalism does not enjoy wide support. In fact, no other constitutional option attracts such broad approval, or rather the prospect of broad approval (in principle if not in every detail) from Left and Right (and centre), Nationalist and Unionist. And it is not difficult to see why, for it is the only constitutional model that would give adequate and coherent expression to the delightfully messy status quo.

I say 'delightfully' but that should not indicate approval. The United Kingdom of Great Britain and Northern Ireland is a very odd country, a product of geography, history and pragmatic constitutionalism. Its head of state is a monarch with two religions, responsible for the appointment of one central government and three devolved administrations as well as three self-governing Crown Dependencies. On top of that it somehow copes with three legal systems, four education systems, two established churches (and none in Wales) and a myriad of different electoral systems and modes of local government.

And as presently constituted it is a little over 90 years old, which gives lie to Nationalist claims that it is somehow singularly inflexible and unreformable. On the contrary, what is now a multi-layered Union of three and a half nations has proved remarkably elastic since England first absorbed (or annexed) Wales in the mid 16th century. Nevertheless that is where we find ourselves in 2014 but, as Harold Macmillan realised more than 50 years ago, the key issue is 'interdependence' rather than contrived visions of 'independence' or nostalgic conceptions of 'the Union'.

As the veteran political scientist Richard Rose pondered in his 2014 memoir, *Learning About Politics in Time and Space* (ECPR Press), the 'alternatives of independence and devolution are inadequate; the key concept is interdependence'. He continued:

> The United Kingdom institutionalises interdependence in a multi-national Westminster Parliament in which Scotland has some seats but England has more. What happens in Brussels or Beijing can have more impact on all parts of the United Kingdom than what happens at Westminster. The cross-national interdependencies arising from globalisation diminish England's claim to be a big fish by increasing the size of the pond. In the words of a former Belgian prime minister, 'There are two kinds of countries in the world today: those that are small and know it and those that are small and don't'.

The choice facing Scots in 2014, Rose added, 'is between alternative forms of interdependence'. And while, he argued, emphasising the uncertainties of independence 'may see off the threat of a Scottish majority endorsing independence', it would 'not address the problem of what to do about the decline in confidence in government in England. Nor does it address the challenge posed by former American Secretary of State Dean Acheson in 1962: 'Britain has lost an Empire but has yet to find a role.'

The main driver of constitutional change in Scotland at the moment, the Scottish National Party, increasingly hints – sometimes explicitly – at what it calls a 'confederal' arrangement, an obvious attempt to square the circle of what, with all its intellectual contortions, has been dubbed 'independence-lite'. The SNP also stresses *interdependence* rather than old-fashioned 19th-century *independence*, and rightly so; Alex Salmond has said (with my italics) that the 'resumption of independence is the resumption of political and economic *sovereignty*. How you then *choose to exercise that sovereignty* reflects the inter-relationships with principally the other countries in these islands.' But I would contend that the logical response to the interdependent reality of the modern, globalised world, is not independence as defined by the SNP, but federalism.

Just as federalist governance of Europe and defence (as described, approvingly, by Acheson in his 1962 speech) has offered the UK an often grudging role on the world stage, federalism could reboot the role of Great Britain (and Northern Ireland) in the domestic arena. Importantly, both sides in the independence debate now accept the realities of multi-level governance split between Brussels, London and Edinburgh, although of course they differ as to the extent of each. But only a federal settlement can hope to give adequate expression to this interdependent reality, particularly in social, political and fiscal terms: 'independence' would lead to a democratic deficit in reverse, with the UK government and Parliament responsible for energy market, currency, etc, without any Scottish representation, while further ad hoc devolution would not address the anomalies inherent in the status quo, giving rise to several more West Lothian Questions and leaving the important issue of English governance unresolved.

This is not to say the UK is somehow a 'failed' state or 'ramshackle' Union, a caricature beloved of Nairnite Nationalists, for it clearly functions relatively well, but constitutionally it is undoubtedly subject to the law of diminishing returns. And nor would federalism be a panacea; even federations carry their own anomalies and imperfections (as illustrated by Belgium), but it is the best system, as David Melding has argued, 'to synthesise the liberal demands of nationalism with those of the Union'. After all federalism, as JAR Marriott observed in the late 19th century, is 'essentially a compromise', and so it would be in the early 21st century between the seemingly irreconcilable tribes of Unionism and Nationalism.

In other words a federal state would enable the UK's four Home Nations to do their own thing within mutually agreed constraints while also answering the much-neglected English Question. It would also represent the logical conclusion of the current direction of travel in Scotland, Wales, Northern Ireland, London and the regions of England, under which more and more powers are being devolved downwards from Westminster. Although this is being done in an ad hoc and therefore incoherent manner, it is nevertheless incrementally nudging the UK towards becoming more and more federal.

As the historian Ben Jackson has argued, if the late Sir Neil MacCormick was correct in his analysis that we live in an age of 'post-sovereignty' then devolution – and, I would argue, federalism – expresses that spirit quite well, 'with decisions about Scottish affairs already diffused across Edinburgh, London and Brussels'. As he added:

There is certainly scope for debate about how best to distribute responsibilities between these three levels of government, but the removal of Scottish representation from London, while still relying on London's goodwill in fundamental domains of public policy, would be an abrupt and rather fraught departure from these promising new constitutional arrangements.

Now Alex Salmond, of course, talks the language of interdependency but ends up reaching the wrong conclusion. And interestingly, when recently asked 'wouldn't federalism be a nice idea', he responded by saying 'their timing is slightly late', thus suggesting his objection was one of tardiness rather than any fundamental philosophical disagreement.

And although he had a point – federalists have often been far too timid in making their case – it was telling that the man leading the campaign for a 'yes' vote did not dismiss federalism out of hand. Indeed, the independence referendum masterminded by Scotland and the SNP leader has turned out to be a very useful prism through which to examine how the United Kingdom is governed while presenting Unionists (and federalists) with an opportunity to explain themselves; and, as I have argued, during that long debate it has become clear that neither independence, with all its intellectual contortions, nor the devolutionary status quo, with all its untidiness, is fit for purpose.

Such a view is not a new one, for a federal solution to the governance of the UK is as old as the modern constitutional debate – inaugurated by the Liberal split over Irish Home Rule in 1886. Even the ostensibly pro-independence thinker Tom Nairn, in his 1977 book *The Break-Up of Britain*, advocated 'building up a new, fairer, more federal British order' as opposed to the 'dingy, fearful compromise' of 'devolution', and also wrote approvingly of 'an Association of British States as the successor to the United Kingdom', preserving what was 'functional' or 'viable' in the Union via 'negotiated agreements among the constituent parts'.

Although frustration with any tangible progress towards a federal UK is entirely understandable, the post-1999 devolutionary settlement has produced an increasingly federal system of government, just as the relationship between the 1921–72 Northern Ireland Parliament (Stormont) and Westminster was federal in nature, so too is that between the devolved parliaments and assemblies of Scotland, Wales, Northern Ireland and London. As the 2009 Calman Commission report noted, Scotland 'relates to the UK Government in many of the same ways as a state government would to a federal one'.

UK governance since 1885, meanwhile, has been much caricatured, but in truth has never been uniform in an administrative sense. As the political scientist Michael Keating observed, its 'multi-national nature' had 'always carried federal implications and created some tension with the centralist Westminster regime'. But one thing is clear: since 1999 the UK has experienced federalism by stealth, so why not formalise it? After all, the leap between the quasi-federal status quo and a formal UK federation is much shorter than that between ad hoc devolution and independence as defined by the SNP. In other words, theory has to catch up with the constitutional reality.

Of course, cynics will argue that federalism is only presently being discussed because independence is in prospect and that is true, up to a point, yet even so that hardly makes the proposition a frivolous one. And besides, for those with longer memories, the federalist case is not merely an opportunistic response to contemporary events but has much deeper roots. As outlined in Chapter 1, the UK came very close to pursuing such a course in the 1910s and 1920s but pulled back as the Irish Question was seemingly resolved; thereafter it was often discussed, usually by Liberals, but with little practical progress.

Federalism would also be consistent with the pragmatic UK constitutional tradition, and arguably in keeping with a related Scottish provenance, from Fletcher of Saltoun's original conception of the 1707 Act of Union to the thinking – albeit incomplete – of Scottish constitutional reformers over the past half century. To argue, as many do, that federalism is not worth contemplating because 'it isn't going to happen', what then was the case for Scottish independence until the early 1960s when it too looked far-fetched? It is an acutely conservative argument. Without meaning to sound complacent (and no federalist can afford that indulgence), when soberly considered none of the arguments *against* federalism are compelling or insurmountable, yet federalism remains, to quote David Melding again, 'something of an f-word in British political discourse'.

But just as another more colourful 'f' word has increasingly become an acceptable fixture of modern cultural life, so too should its constitutional equivalent. If the UK wanted to become a federal parliamentary state it could do so without serious disruption to its traditional political culture. And while no one can pretend such a transition would be easy, it is a vision worth pursuing, not only as an end in itself but also as a means to better outcomes in other important aspects of public policy. To paraphrase Victor Hugo, an unreformed Union might be able to resist pro-independence armies for several decades to come, but federalism is an old idea whose time has finally come.

Some other books published by **Luath Press**

100 Days of Hope and Fear
David Torrance
ISBN 978 1 910021 31 6 PBK £9.99

The People's Referendum: Why Scotland Will Never Be the Same Again
Peter Geoghegan
ISBN 978-1-910021-52-1 PBK £9.99

Reading this diary back during the editing process it was clear that, like (Nate) Silver (the US polling guru whose view was that the Yes campaign had virtually no chance of victory), I got a lot of things wrong (including the likely margin of victory) but also many things broadly correct. At least I can plead, as journalists often do, that I was probably right at the time.

What can the people of Scotland – and other aspirant nations – learn from this seismic democratic event? Scotland's independence referendum on 18 September 2014 was the most significant ballot in Scotland's history. The 100 days up to 18 September was the official campaign period and the world's media was watching. David Torrance was there throughout, in front of the cameras, on the radio, in the newspapers, at the debates and gatherings, privy to some of the behind-the-scenes manoeuvrings.

A passionate federalist at heart, described disparagingly by the outgoing First Minister as 'Tory-leaning', Torrance made a valiant attempt to remain 'professionally neutral' throughout. His commentary and analysis, as the campaign went through its many twists and turns, was always insightful, if not always popular.

This book is about how the independence referendum changed not just Scottish politics but the nation's people, its sense of itself and its future. This is the story of the campaign and its aftermath, not as recorded by pollsters and politicians, but as it was experienced by some of the five million ordinary – and extraordinary – people involved on both sides of the debate. Their stories also speak to what comes next for Scotland.

19 September 2014. The ballots are in, the votes counted. Scotland has chosen to remain part of the UK. The result is black and white, but the journey to it is anything but monochrome. For months Scots discussed their futures, in town halls and living rooms across the land. The debate gripped the nation like no other in Scottish history. Full of character, and characters, this lively, in-depth book provides a unique perspective on a referendum that will reshape Scotland for years to come.

A unique and challenging perspective on the year that changed Scotland.
LIBBY BROOKS

A generous, original and distinctive take on Scottish national life.
JAMIE MAXWELL

Peter Geoghegan has succinctly and astutely identified the heart of the matter.
WILL STORRAR

Great Scottish Speeches Vol. 1
Introduced and Edited by David Torrance
Foreword by Alex Salmond
ISBN 978 1 906817 27 4 PBK £9.99

Great Scottish Speeches Vol. 2
Introduced and Edited by David Torrance
Foreword by Alex Salmond
ISBN 978 1 908373 63 2 HBK £16.99

Some great Scottish speeches were the result of years of contemplation. Some flourished in heat of the moment. Whatever the background of the ideas expressed, the speeches not only provide a snapshot of their time, but express views that still resonate in Scotland today, whether you agree with the sentiments or not.

Encompassing speeches made by Scots or in Scotland, this carefully selected collection reveals the character of a nation. Themes of religion, independence and socialism cross paths with sporting encouragement, Irish Home Rule and Miss Jean Brodie.

Ranging from the legendary speech of the Caledonian chief Calgagus in 83AD right up to Alex Salmond's election victory in 2007, these are the speeches that created modern Scotland.

...what has not faded is the power of the written and spoken word – as this first-rate collection of Scottish speeches demonstrates.
PRESS AND JOURNAL

Following on the success of *Great Scottish Speeches*, Vol. 1 and ahead of the potentially radical changes to our political landscape after the referendum next year, David Torrance once again delves into the archives of Scottish public speaking to compile a second volume of memorable and inspirational speeches.

Featuring speeches from some of the most well-known and memorable speakers in Scottish history, *Great Scottish Speeches*, Vol. 2 is a worthy successor to his first collection. Not restricted to purely political oratories, Torrance shares with us a broad range of addresses from celebrated poets, musicians and writers with each speech being framed by an introduction, setting out its historical importance and contextualising what is to follow.

As Scotland embarks on a new process of discussion and debate about our constitutional future, it is timely to celebrate the different voices and strands of opinion which have taken the nation to our present place – and to encourage new voices for our future progress. Let the discourse begin!
ALEX SALMOND

Details of these and other books published by Luath Press can be found at
www.luath.co.uk

Luath Press Limited

committed to publishing well written books worth reading

LUATH PRESS takes its name from Robert Burns, whose little collie
Luath (*Gael.*, swift or nimble) tripped up Jean Armour at a wedding
and gave him the chance to speak to the woman who was to be his wife
and the abiding love of his life. Burns called one of the 'Twa Dogs'
Luath after Cuchullin's hunting dog in Ossian's *Fingal*.
Luath Press was established in 1981 in the heart of
Burns country, and is now based a few steps up
the road from Burns' first lodgings on
Edinburgh's Royal Mile. Luath offers you
distinctive writing with a hint of
unexpected pleasures.
Most bookshops in the UK, the US, Canada,
Australia, New Zealand and parts of Europe,
either carry our books in stock or can order them
for you. To order direct from us, please send a £sterling
cheque, postal order, international money order or your
credit card details (number, address of cardholder and
expiry date) to us at the address below. Please add post
and packing as follows: UK – £1.00 per delivery address;
overseas surface mail – £2.50 per delivery address; overseas airmail –
£3.50 for the first book to each delivery address, plus £1.00 for each
additional book by airmail to the same address. If your order is a gift,
we will happily enclose your card or message at no extra charge.

Luath Press Limited
543/2 Castlehill
The Royal Mile
Edinburgh EH1 2ND
Scotland
Telephone: +44 (0)131 225 4326 (24 hours)
Fax: +44 (0)131 225 4324
email: sales@luath. co.uk
Website: www. luath.co.uk